Joe,
Another beautiful river! Best regards.
Tim

Joe—
River environments
= a " us!
Dave L

D0282475

A COMMON TRAGEDY: HISTORY OF AN URBAN RIVER

Timothy J. Iannuzzi
David F. Ludwig
Jason C. Kinnell
Jennifer M. Wallin
William H. Desvousges
Richard W. Dunford

Amherst Scientific Publishers

ACKNOWLEDGMENTS

The development of this book, which is based on the compilation and synthesis of thousands of pieces of historical information collected from a variety of sources, would not have been possible without the help and advice of many people. First, we would like to thank Kimberlee McIntyre for her hard work in the preparation and editing of this book, and for her careful (sometimes painful) coordination between the six co-authors. We would also like to thank our colleagues at BBL Sciences and TER for their various contributions to this work.

We would like to extend our gratitude to Paul Kostecki and Betty Niedzwiecki of the Association for Environmental Health and Sciences (AEHS), and Amherst Scientific Publishers, for encouraging and fostering the publication of this book. Special thanks also to Charles F. Cummings, the Assistant Director for Special Collections at the Newark Public Library and Newark City Historian, for all his guidance and help in obtaining many of the images and historic articles that proved so valuable to this work, and for reviewing the manuscript and writing the forward. Also, we would like to thank the staff at the New Jersey Historical Society and Newark Public Library for their kind help with our research. Last, but not least, we would like to extend our sincere appreciation and gratitude to Tierra Solutions, Inc. for providing the funding to conduct the countless hours of research that went into this book.

FOREWORD

The rise and fall, and rise again of an American river is the theme of *A Common Tragedy: History of An Urban River.* This work traces historical events along a waterway in one of our nation's most congested metropolitan centers. The authors investigate the delicate dance between man and environment from pre-history through the events of today. In many instances, the magnitude of some of these events could not be fully recognized until a historical survey such as this laid them out for the modern reader.

This "Passaic River" study is scholarly with scores of charts, lists, chronologies, footnotes, and a rich bibliography for the specialist. Still, the text "flows" for the average reader as well. From the earliest geological and historical descriptions the reader is transported through time to the beginning of reconstitution of a "dead" or the "second worst polluted river in America" into a recovering and rediscovered asset. Newark and the more than three hundred communities that line the Passaic's shores have benefited and taken from it for generations, and are beginning to look at the River as a major resource in their 21st century redevelopment. Lessons taken from the waterfront revivals of other major cities such as Baltimore and San Antonio are being heeded. The cycle of life emerging from water may well be re-enacted on the Passaic River today.

The Native American, Dutch, English, and later the Connecticut Puritans found the Passaic River essential to 17th and 18th century progress. The 19th and 20th century manufacturers, travelers, and sports persons used the River it for their own individual goals. In the wake of these activities the Passaic River nearly died and was forgotten. Still, life is returning to the River and with new energy.

Topics included in this Passaic River compendium include its geological and historical past; the role of the Dutch, English, and American developers; the changes in shoreline and wetlands over three centuries; and the role of industrialization an urbanism. All phases of recreation have been visited and the final question asked—have we learned from past mistakes? This is recommended reading for admirers of rivers in general and the Passaic in particular.

Charles F. Cummings
Assistant Director for Special Collections,
  Newark Public Library
Newark City Historian

CONTENTS

1

UNDERSTANDING URBAN ECOSYSTEMS
A Tragic Past and Uncertain Future

"The future of the earth is entwined with the human race."

K.N. Lee (1993)

SCIENTISTS AND REGULATORS around the world want to restore degraded ecosystems. This desire is pronounced in industrial and urban regions, including the major metropolitan areas of the United States. While restoration ecology is still a developing science, it is being applied, along with economics and engineering, as a management tool for natural resource restoration. Where theory meets application, the process of ecological restoration becomes difficult. Success is uncertain, and costs can be high. They must be weighed against the benefits of successful restoration, both in terms of ecology and human use of natural resources. The restoration process itself must be built on a solid foundation that includes historical perspective and the best science. Most importantly, we must understand the current condition of the resource and the circumstances that led to its degradation. Only then can we make the value judgements needed to plan successful restoration.

Evaluating the condition of natural resources in urban areas requires an understanding of both historical and current ecology and land use. It is also important to understand the economics behind environmental changes, including why and how people altered resources through time. It is not enough to count organisms, classify habitats, and characterize human uses today, and assume that this snapshot can support wise decisions on resource management or restoration. We need to delve deeper into the history of the resource and the services it provides. We must address how humans have used the resource and the effects of that use. Only then can we begin to manage and restore the environment in a balanced way that accounts for present and future human needs while maximizing ecosystem benefits, including habitat quality and biodiversity.

This book presents a case study on the historical ecology and economics of an urban river system in Newark, New Jersey; a city in the heart of one of the most industrialized metropolitan ecosystems in the world—the New York/New Jersey (NY/NJ) Harbor Estuary. This region and its Estuary have grown from Native American settlements and small 17th and 18th century colonial waterfront villages to one of the world's busiest cities and industrial ports. Several previous works have chronicled the settlement, development, and industrialization of the NY/NJ Harbor Estuary. Among them are John Kieran's *A Natural History of New York City* (1959), Robert Boyle's *The Hudson River: A Natural and Unnatural History* (1969), David Pierson's *Narratives of Newark* (1917), Paul Cohen and Robert Augustyn's *Manhattan in Maps, 1527–1995* (1997), Peter Wacker and Paul Clemen's *Land Use in Early New Jersey: A Historical Geography* (1995), Kevin Bone's *The New York Waterfront: Evolution and Building Culture of the Port and Harbor* (1997), and John Cunningham's *Newark* (1988). Each of these books is well worth reading for a more in-depth perspective on localized areas or waterways within the Estuary.

Our focus is on a highly industrialized stretch of one of the major tributaries of the NY/NJ Harbor Estuary—the lower portion of the Passaic River. The River (upstream of its confluence with Newark Bay) has served the needs of a rapidly growing human population and industrial expansion in the city of Newark for nearly two centuries (Figure 1-1). The lower Passaic River is a prime example of resource degradation at its worst. But, as will be seen, there is hope for its future.

The River has been the subject of recent scientific and regulatory investigations regarding types, amounts, and sources of pollution from industrial and municipal sources (e.g., Beale, 1972; NJDEP, 1987; Wenning *et al.*, 1994; NY/NJ HEP, 1996; Iannuzzi *et al.*, 1997; Huntley *et al.*, 1997; Walker *et al.*, 1999). The ultimate objective is to determine an appropriate "fix" for the "problem" of pollution, to improve the health of the ecosystem, and increase human use of the River. Our goal in this book is to provide a framework for understanding the relative importance of the many factors behind the current condition of the River, allowing us to put the role of industrial pollution in the greater context of the full array of historical impacts.

3

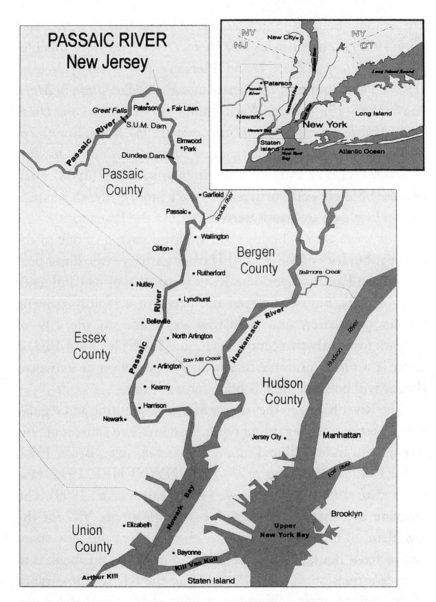

Figure 1-1. The Passaic River and NY/NJ Harbor Estuary

Urban ecosystems like the Passaic River provide a new challenge to the paradigms on which ecologists base their investigations. The Passaic has not been a "pristine" resource for more than two centuries. While its ecology is dynamic, it can never be returned to its primeval state. Therefore, we humans, the stakeholders in and stewards of the River and its resources, must make value judgements as to what is the "right," "appropriate," or "correct" ecological restoration. Our judgements must be based on a balanced assessment of the actions needed to restore impaired service functions of the River's resources, yet support the expanding needs of a growing population in the Newark metropolitan area. This analysis requires a holistic understanding of urban ecology, including, to the extent possible, a detailed characterization of the succession of ecological conditions at varying levels of degradation.

For whatever reason, ecologists have, until very recently, focused their research on relatively pristine places, rather than resources that have been obviously affected by humans (Ludwig, 1989). An examination of basic ecology textbooks from the decades when the science of ecology was being formulated is very enlightening. Some, like Pianka (1974), devote a single chapter to a discussion of man and his environment. Others, like Odum (1963) and Boughey (1971), could spare only a few pages for the place of humans in the biosphere. For the most part, the principles, examples, and conclusions of fundamental ecological research are based on analysis of systems with as little overt human influence as possible. With this foundation, ecology as a way of understanding the holistic interactions between earth and its inhabitants has been hampered by the presumption of a dichotomous world: parts of the biosphere that have people and

5

parts that do not. The presumption then is that the parts of the biosphere affected by people should look like the parts that are not.

The problem with this view, of course, is that few (if any) places on earth have escaped the influence of humans (Ludwig, 1985). Our reference conditions are confounded with our test conditions, and nothing is pristine. Humans have been actively and drastically altering the biosphere for thousands, probably tens of thousands, of years.

In contrast, economists focus almost exclusively on the parts of the biosphere clearly influenced by humans. Economics is the study of resource constraints on human decisions. Economics assumes that people make choices to maximize their well-being within a constrained environment. The choices people make reveal trade-offs showing the relative "value" of alternatives. By addressing these trade-offs, economics provides a counter point to the ecological approach that assumes the reference condition to be "pristine." Thus, economics offers a useful complement to ecology, helping to integrate understanding of the role of people and their preferences in the biosphere.

Fundamentally, there is an "evolutionary" relationship between humans and the environment. Humans use the environment, modifying it and changing the ability of people to use it in the future. This feedback loop is important and has only become clear as multidisciplinary syntheses of information from archaeology, history, ecology, evolutionary biology, geology, and environmental chemistry have developed. A seminal work in this great synthesis is *Changes in the Land: Indians, Colonists, and the Ecology of New England* by William Cronon (1983). Through painstaking reconstruction of diverse records of New England from prehistoric times through European settlement, Cronon demonstrated the important role that aboriginal peoples played in altering the landscape of the eastern United States. Using similar research methods and a single theme, Stephen Pyne (1997a, b,c; 1998) has shown how fire, often in the nominal service of people, has modified ecosystems around the globe for millennia. An accessible account of the effect of native Americans on the North American continent as a whole is provided in *The Ecological Indian: Myth and History* (Krech, 1999). Global syntheses (not always presented with scientific dispassion, but containing a wealth of information and interesting conclusions) about man as a force in the biosphere include *A Green History of the World: The Environment and the Collapse of Great Civilizations* by Clive Ponting (1991), *Ecological Imperialism: The Biological Expansion of Europe, 900–1900* and *The Colombian Exchange: Biological and Cultural Consequences of 1492* by Alfred Crosby (1986 and 1972, respectively). The meaning of all the rapidly accumulating data on human ecology has been described (Eisenberg, 1998) and debated (Myers and Simon, 1994). But it is now quite clear that human beings have been a major determinant of environmental conditions for a long time, and that human modification of the biosphere has accelerated in the past few centuries.

The complex and ever-changing relationship between people and natural resources leaves us with a dilemma for environmental assessment. In the absence of true reference sites, how can we identify, let alone quantify, the incremental impact of a single factor? In particular, how can we apportion impacts among the myriad possible sources? While this problem is global in nature, it is certainly more acute for highly urbanized environments like the Passaic River. The fundamental question is: what tractable parameter can we use as a standard against which to measure site- and time-specific impacts associated with particular human activities?

The answer is found in the concept of "baseline." Identifying the baseline condition of a resource involves determining how that resource would look and function but for the effect in question, and only that effect. This "but for" baseline incorporates both the environmental conditions themselves and the human uses that depend on those conditions. For example, to determine the effect of a given chemical release into a river ecosystem, we must first assess what the river's ecosystem would have looked like at this point in history if everything in its history had occurred except for the release in question. All other human effects, such as dredging for navigation, road construction, agricultural run-off, wetlands draining, and others are parts of the baseline condition, thereby isolating the effect of the release. The baseline also affects the services provided by the resource. These services may include functions provided to other resources, known as ecological services, or functions provided to humans, known as human-use services. A change in the characteristics of the river will alter the services it provides, thereby altering how people use the river. Thus, the human-use feedback loop, integrating economics and ecology, is explicitly included in any evaluation of environmental baseline.

The fundamental tool of baseline analysis is historical reconstruction, synthesizing available data to piece together a chronology of the resource's characteristics and uses. Such data are likely to include both technical measurements, such as counts of organisms, concentrations of chemicals, and intensity of physical forces, and written records of conditions and uses over time. By analyzing such information, we can determine the "but for" condition: how would the resource function but for the impact in question?

This book provides an example of a historical reconstruction for the Passaic River. Through a detailed compilation and analysis of historical information on the Passaic and its adjacent watershed, we have attempted to re-construct the conditions of this river and its services from pre-Columbian times to the present. At the same time, we have documented and characterized the environmental degradation of the River's once bountiful natural resources, and the corresponding changes in services (Figure 1-2). Habitat destruction, wetlands drainage, land alterations, hazardous chemical releases, and garbage and sewage disposal represent key impacts to this system since the Industrial Revolution.

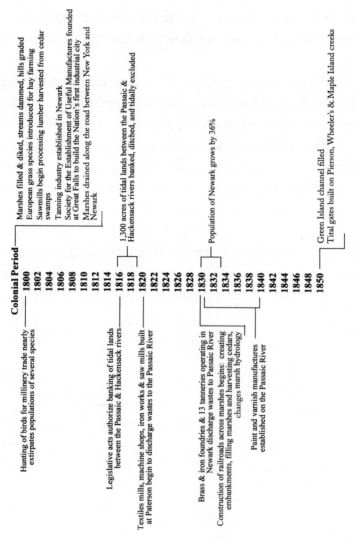

Figure 1-2. Historical timeline of environmental degradation of the Passaic River and Newark Bay (Colonial Period–present)

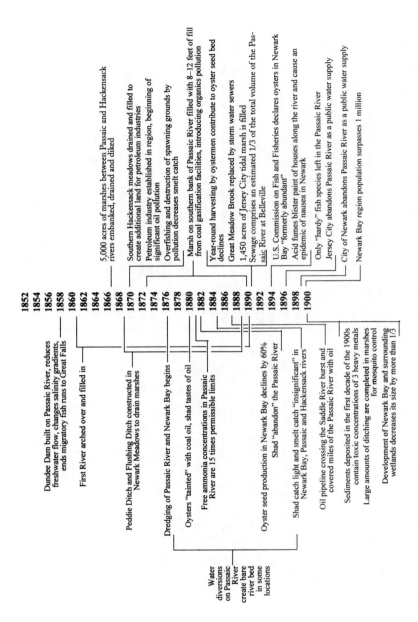

Figure 1-2. (continued)

11

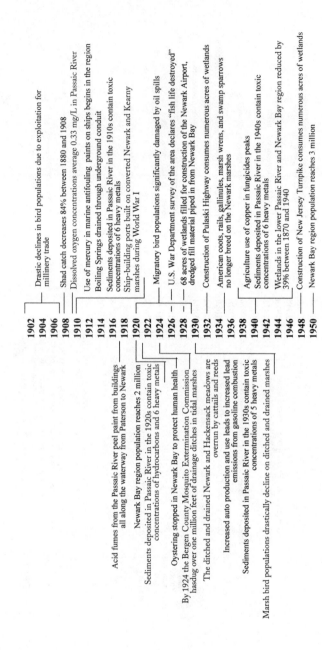

Figure 1-2. (continued)

12

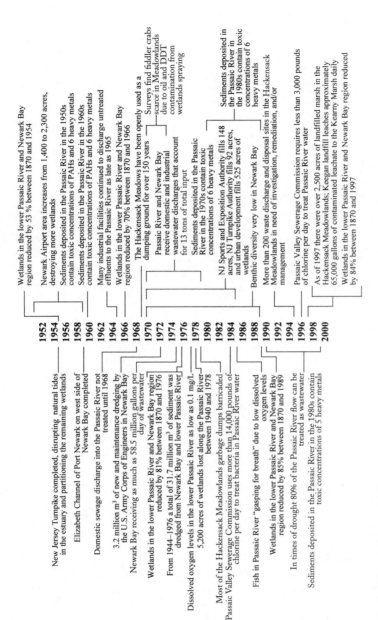

Figure 1-2. (continued)

2
ECOLOGY AND ECONOMICS
Tools for Regulation and Management

"Many will be surprised to learn that a considerable difference of opinion exists regarding what is—and what is not—a damage."

R.J. Kopp and V.K. Smith (1993)

BUILDING A HISTORICAL PICTURE of a resource and its services has two implicit objectives: understanding how things got where they are, and showing the path forward. The need to understand how a resource reached its present state often stems from regulation (or the lack thereof), and the associated need to assess the degree and extent of environmental degradation. The other half of the story, the path into the future, arises from the need to make effective management decisions for the recovery of the resource. Both of these objectives rely on sound ecological and economic research.

15

Environmental Assessment: How Did We Get Here?

Laws regulating waterway pollution existed in England in the fourteenth century, and proliferated during the Industrial Revolution. The need for these laws grew from the fundamental economic concept of "externalities." Economic analysis is often based on the assumption that markets will allocate society's resources efficiently, including labor, capital, and natural resources (Smith, 1937). This assumption, however, is only valid if all assets have well-defined private property rights (Coase, 1960). That is, all resources involved in a market have a clear owner who bears all benefits and costs for the use of that resource. Resources that do not have private property rights create a market "failure" and the market misallocates resources. This failure occurs when the operation of the market generates effects that are "external" to the market.

A general example is in the manufacture of widgets resulting in the release of chemicals into a nearby river. Widgets are traded in a market where producers and consumers interact to set a price and a production level. However, chemical releases are outside the market—they are "external." The manufacturer bears no costs from chemical release "production." The manufacturer does not rent the space in the river where the chemicals end up. The manufacturer pays no compensation to the users of the river who now experience reduced river services. There is no market mechanism to ensure that the river resource is used efficiently. Regulations, therefore, were developed as a reaction to these "externalities." The goal of these regulations was to repair the market failure that led to the degradation of unpriced, public resources. Whether or not regulations meet this goal remains an open question.

In the U.S., federal and state environmental regulations were published throughout the latter half of the 19th century and first half of the 20th century. The effectiveness of these laws was constrained by a lack of specific standards or assessment benchmarks against which to measure compliance (Percival *et al.*, 1992). This situation changed in the 1970s. With the promulgation of the National Environmental Policy Act ("NEPA," 1970), the Water Pollution Control Act ("Clean Water Act," 1972), the Marine Protection, Research and Sanctuaries Act ("Ocean Dumping Act," 1972), and the Endangered Species Act (1973), technical assessment of environmental conditions was integrated into the decision making process.

NEPA in particular generated specific assessment protocols to support decisions about proposed activities that might impact the environment. A typical assessment examines the affected environment, expected impacts, the regulatory context in which the decision must be made, and a range of alternative actions. NEPA assessments also typically include at least a qualitative discussion of socioeconomic effects. The success of the NEPA assessment process as a decision tool has been questioned (Moran and Limburg, 1986). Nevertheless, this process is the first truly formal and fundamental approach to rigorous environmental assessment. In many ways, assessments under other regulatory programs owe their technical foundations to the NEPA approach.

In 1980, the Comprehensive Environmental Response, Compensation, and Liability Act (CERCLA, or "Superfund") established environmental assessment as a foundation for cleaning up hazardous-substance releases. Following the 1986 Superfund Amendments and Reauthorization Act, extensive guidance was prepared on the technical process for Superfund environmental assessment. Much of the regulatory and technical foundation of Superfund is oriented to human health and ecological toxicology, as hazardous-substance releases are the focus of the legislation. However, a provision in the Act for recovering natural resource damages brings the condition of ecosystems and the interaction with economics into focus.

Natural resource damage assessments (NRDAs) evaluate the environmental impacts caused by hazardous-substances releases that are not addressed by direct environmental remediation.[1] The assessment determines what services have been diminished by these releases, and calculates the value of those services "foregone." Under CERCLA, the "responsible party" (responsible for the chemical release) must reimburse the public for the services lost while the resource was in a degraded state due to the specific chemical release. This reimbursement may come in the form of monetary or environmental compensation. In addition, the responsible party must restore the resource to its baseline condition. Baseline, as discussed in Chapter 1, refers to the condition of the resource but for the specific release, not the pristine condition that may have existed without any human influence.

As a hypothetical example, consider a wetland near an industrial facility that processes metals. Before the industrial facility was built, portions of the wetland were filled in a misguided attempt to "reclaim" them. Then, with the operation of the industrial facility, some metals leaked into the remaining wetland area, settling into the sediment. After some years, the leak is discovered and halted, and the metals in the environment are addressed

---

[1] NRDAs are also performed for oil spills, but these assessments are regulated under the Oil Pollution Act ("OPA," 1990), not CERCLA.

18

by risk-based cleanup. Cleanup actions may include some sediments being removed or capped if health risks to people and the ecosystem are high, while others may be left in place if risks are low. These remediation actions are explicitly aimed at ending the exposure and minimizing risks.

These remediation actions do not address any impacts to natural resources that might have occurred over the intervening years resulting from these leaks. Instead, the NRDA assesses these effects. The assessment begins with determining what resource services have been diminished because of the leaks. For example, fish reproduction might have been suppressed, leaving lower populations to support recreational activities or to provide food for fish-eating birds. The remaining fish may not be safe for people to eat because of metal contamination, thereby diminishing the enjoyment people get from fishing in the area. Wetland plant productivity might have been reduced, or bottom-dwelling invertebrates (key components of the ecosystem) might have been subject to chronic stress and reduced abundance and diversity.

The key aspect of the NRDA process is the requirement for quantifying incremental damages associated solely with a hazardous-substance release. NRDA regulations and guidance are very explicit on this point. Incremental damages are those that are attributable to the specific hazardous-substance release after all other aspects of environmental condition have been considered. In our example, therefore, diminished productivity of the wetland resulting from the earlier filling activity is not compensible as a part of NRDA. Only the effects stemming directly from the release of metals are relevant. It is a challenging task to separate the effects of specific hazardous substances from other environmental impacts in a highly urbanized river like the Passaic. Developing a detailed historical picture of the ecology and economics of the resource is one tool that can be applied to meet this challenge.

Managing the Environment

The NRDA process is not simply an enforcement exercise. The main objective of the damage assessment component of Superfund is restoration, a forward-looking action that involves the management of natural resources (e.g., Walz, 1993; NOAA, 1996). In the NRDA context, restoration comes in two forms. First, *primary restoration* entails restoring the affected resource to its baseline condition so that it provides all the resource services it would have provided "but for" the release. So, revisiting our example, primary restoration would restore the waterway to its baseline condition, enabling it to provide services, such as fishing and birdwatching, at a level consistent with baseline. In addition, *compensatory restoration* actions can serve to compensate the public for services lost while the resource was degraded. Thus, to offset the loss of fishing services incurred prior to the restoration of the resource to baseline, management authorities might stock a popular fishing area to make it more productive or might add hiking trails to a popular birdwatching area. These additional services offset the incremental losses incurred as a result of the metal releases.

Compensatory restoration in a highly disturbed urban ecosystem requires creativity as well as good science. The most effective path to restoring lost services may not involve cleaning up the hazardous substances causing the service losses. In urban rivers, factors other than the specific chemical release—such as habitat destruction, watershed modification, changes to the physical environment, or nonpoint pollution—may cause a large share of total environmental impacts. Thus, the best way to restore lost incremental services may be by managing these other factors. The greatest return in increased services is generally possible through the factors causing the greatest impacts. If the incremental losses resulting from chemicals are small relative to losses from other causes, the best restoration actions may involve repairing some of these other factors.

In our example, metals in the sediments may or may not be actively managed based on risk levels. It may not be effective to alter that risk-based decision to address losses in ecological and human use services. Instead, removing some of the historical fill from the wetland may provide new habitat for invertebrates and fish, and so restore many, if not all, the lost services.

It is these complexities—sorting out the most effective paths to resource restoration—that historical ecology and economic analyses can help address. By identifying the baseline services levels in the "but for" world, rational restoration decisions can be made and the most direct and successful management activities undertaken.

3

BEFORE THE EUROPEANS
Who Lived Along the Passaic?

*"For indigenous peoples from the Arctic to the tropics,
there is no wilderness but home."*

F. Berkes (1999)

RIVERS ARE CRITICAL LANDSCAPE FEATURES and vital ecological systems. Throughout history, the world's great civilizations have been built around rivers, which served as the lifeline
for their people's existence. The human services afforded by
rivers include water supply, food production, travel, commerce,
waste removal, and recreation. In addition to its human services,
a river typically provides and supports a wide variety of ecological resources from its headwaters to its confluence with the ocean
or other waterways. Great rivers—those that drain large or diverse watersheds or that offer unique or uniquely valuable ecological and human services—are among the most valuable natural resources on earth. The Passaic was once a great river.

The Passaic River watershed runs from the mountains of New York state through the piedmont of New Jersey to the tidal estuaries of Newark Bay. Before European settlement, the Passaic supported an enormous biological diversity, was a key component of numerous ecological systems, and provided the native peoples with critical environmental and human-use services. While the Passaic's status as a great river has diminished over three centuries of exploitation, it remains an important landscape feature of northeastern New Jersey. In this chapter, we describe what is known or can be surmised about the Passaic River before European colonization, when it was a dominant feature of the region and a key resource for both human and non-human inhabitants. This is the bar against which the following 300 years of impact must be tested—the standard that reveals how far the level of natural resource services fell with the advent of industrialization.

Prehistory

This section summarizes primarily the works of Brydon, *The Passaic River: Past, Present, and Future* (1974), Wright, *The Hackensack Meadowlands: Prehistory and History* (1988), Pierson, *Narratives of Newark* (1917), and Cunningham, *Newark* (1988). These works are fascinating compilations of information from diverse sources on the history of the environmental resources of the Newark region. Each of these publications is well worth reading for their own sakes.

The last glacier receded from the Passaic River watershed about 17,000 years ago, leaving behind the large, cold-water Lake Hackensack (or Lake Passaic, according to Brydon [1974]). The lakeshore and adjacent uplands were inhabited by a diverse fauna of large mammals including mammoths, mastodons, saber-toothed cats, ground sloths, bison, elk, and caribou. About 7,000 years later, the large mammals disappeared at a time when the climate was warming, the vegetation was changing, and early man was beginning to populate the area.

With the milder climate and loss of megafauna, people began to settle into villages on the shores of rivers and estuaries. Little is known about Paleoindians who made the transition from post-glacial times. The life of the Algonquin peoples who followed and inhabited the region for thousands of years prior to Henry Hudson's appearance in the Estuary is better understood.

From about 8,000 to 2,000 years ago, the inhabitants of the Passaic basin were a river people. Their settlements were closely associated with riparian corridors and wetland borders. Fish was an important part of their diet, and they used specialized and effective woven net technology to harvest a variety of species. These people were semi-nomadic, traveling throughout the region to exploit fish and game resources. There was likely an annual or biannual stay in the area of the lower Passaic River and Hackensack Meadowlands to harvest fish, shellfish, and seasonally abundant migratory waterfowl.

Exploitation of estuarine resources began to intensify from around 1000 B.C., to the time of European contact. The Lenape peoples lived in relatively permanent villages throughout the Passaic watershed and raised such crops as maize, beans, squash, fruit, and tobacco. However, in spring, many of the village residents would make an annual trek to the coast to harvest the resources of the lower Passaic and Newark Bay. A relatively small group would remain in the village to husband the crops. By harvest time, the coastal travelers returned and remained in the village until the following spring. This combined system of hunting-gathering and farming supported the small, scattered communities found in the Passaic watershed. Because the villages were small and widely spaced, impact on the watershed was relatively low. This situation may have been unique to the Passaic basin. Elsewhere, the impact of the native Americans in general and the Lenape peoples in particular was greater (Wacker and Clemens, 1995; Russell, 1980). But in the Passaic basin, human impact was low prior to European arrival (Figure 3-1).

Pre-Colonization Environments

In 1705, the total population of New Jersey was estimated to be fewer than 12,000 people, including both European colonists and remnants of the native Lenape peoples (Pierson, 1917; Cunningham, 1988). Prior to that time, and particularly before European settlements began to grow, populations were substantially lower. The landscape of the highland and piedmont through which the Passaic flowed was largely covered in hardwood forest. There is little evidence that the Lenape burned extensively in this area, although they did so farther south (Russell, 1980). The combination of very low population density and low-impact habitation likely assured that there was little degradation of surface water quality because there was little degradation of the forestlands. Relatively undisturbed forested watersheds accumulate nutrients within the terrestrial ecosystems (soils and standing crop of vegetation). Precipitation runoff is less severe in such systems, and sediment transport from the watershed to downstream aquatic ecosystems is low (Morris *et al.*, 1992). Before European settlement, the Passaic River watershed was a landscape able to support surface waters of the highest quality.

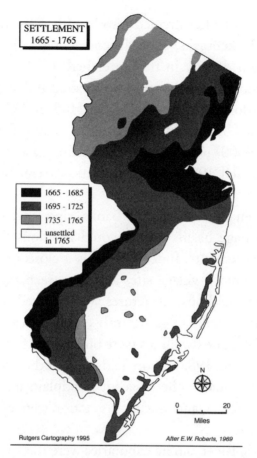

Figure 3-1.   The spread of European colonists throughout New Jersey (Wacker and Clemens, 1995; with permission from the New Jersey Historical Society).

The only major alteration of watersheds by the Lenape peoples was clearing, usually by burning. Cleared, and especially burned areas in watersheds, contribute disproportionately to extreme storm flows and sediment input (Sparks, 1992). However, the Lenape peoples of the Passaic watershed (primarily the

27

Minsi subtribe, further divided into local groups including the Pomptons, Hackensacks, and Musconetcongs) did little burning. Population density in the watershed was low, and groups were scattered. Only small areas were cleared and maintained for planting (Brydon, 1974). Tribes in the Hudson Valley and, further south, the Unami and Unalachtigo Lenape (Brydon, 1974; Bonnicksen, 2000) used large-scale burning as a land-management tool (Russell, 1980). But in the Passaic basin, little land was cleared.

For the Lenape peoples, riverbanks, riparian corridors, and tributary drainage basins were favored locations for the most permanent settlements. Indeed, there is a close spatial correlation between known village sites and the streams (Figure 3-2). Wigwam and longhouse structures were located on level land close to the riverbank but sufficiently elevated to avoid flooding (Brydon, 1974). The dwellings were built of log frames, overlaid with bark (Wright, 1988). Crop fields were at the edge of the village, likely laid out on the adjacent floodplain for appropriate crops. Fish, shellfish, and aquatic vegetation were applied to the fields as fertilizer.

The Passaic River and its tributaries were transportation corridors for the Lenape. They manufactured dugout canoes from various trees, including juniper, cedar, oak, and tulip poplar. They favored red and white cedar for dugouts because of their buoyancy. They constructed lighter, more agile canoes of wood frames with bark skins, which could be used to travel more rapidly (Kalm, 1770).

In general, Lenape technology was based on hand tools and hard work. They cut dugouts from standing trees and hollowed them with glowing coals and shell or stone adzes. They gathered

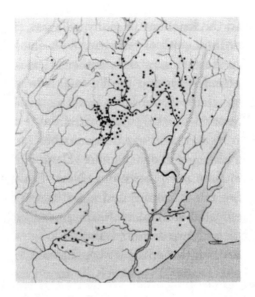

Figure 3-2. Native American settlements in northern New Jersey (with permission from the Newark Museum).

fuel wood by hand and caught fish in nets woven from reeds harvested in riparian wetlands. They cleared crop fields by small-scale burning or by hand cutting of existing vegetation. They stripped trees to provide bark for canoes and dwellings, hunted game, often in areas remote from the village proper, and maintained croplands. Overall, it is likely that the per capita impact on the waterways and riparian ecosystems was low.

Population densities were extremely low in the Passaic River basin prior to European colonization. It has been estimated that there were between eight and ten thousand Lenape in all of New Jersey at the time of European contact (Kraft, 1986). If this population was divided equally among the three Lenape tribes, there would have been no more than two or three thousand people living in the Passaic River basin at this time. In fact, an early report estimates that there were about one thousand Hackensacks in 1643 (Brodhead, 1953). Assuming that the three subtribes of the Minsi were each about the same size, this would mean about three thousand people occupying the entire Passaic River basin, with a seasonal migration of most of the people to the coast at the NY/NJ Harbor Estuary. Given the low environmental impact per individual, it is likely that the wetlands, woodlands, and waterways of the Passaic River drainage were largely intact and relatively undisturbed when European colonists arrived in the region.

Farming came late to the Lenape, probably not before the Late Woodland Period between about 1000 B.C. and 1600 A.D. Until then, all three tribes depended on what they could hunt and gather from the woodlands and riverways in spring and autumn and the estuaries in summer (Kraft, 1986). This meant a diet consisting largely of foraged fruits, nuts, and roots with fish, shellfish, and game (some of it preserved for winter use) as a major source of protein (Brydon, 1974). The various ecosystems of the Passaic River basin and associated estuaries supported an enormous variety of fish, shellfish, and wildlife resources. On a seasonal basis, the Lenape harvested migratory birds, wintering and breeding birds, deer, small mammals of various species, turtles, frogs, fish, shellfish, and native plants (Kraft, 1986). Migratory birds and anadromous fish (such as herrings, shad, sturgeon, and salmon) and catadromous fish (eels) were particularly important in the annual diet.

There is little direct evidence of the fish and wildlife resources of the Passaic River prior to European colonization. However, the breadth of the Lenape diet, coupled with the low population density and seasonal migration patterns, suggests that the landscape as a whole provided abundant services via these resources. The natural resource services baseline was likely not greatly affected by the few thousand Lenape inhabitants of the area through the 17th century. It was only when population densities increased under the pressure of European colonization that the area's ecosystems began to degrade.

4

THE EUROPEANS
How was the Passaic
Used and Abused?

"No one who knows the Passaic from the Paterson or Newark waterfront could possibly imagine that the stream was once a waterway of delight . . ."

H.E. Wildes (1943)

THE DUTCH WERE PROBABLY the first Europeans to explore the Passaic River. While Verrazano, Gomez, and Hudson all visited the NY/NJ Harbor Estuary, there is no record of the Passaic in any maps or accounts of their voyages (e.g., Lunny, 1959). But the Dutch, through their Manhattan Island trading depot, likely traveled to the Passaic seeking furs and other commercial goods. They established a post at Bergen in 1618, beginning the westward expansion of European settlement. The Dutch soon purchased much of the land between the Hudson and Hackensack Rivers from the Indians (Urquart, 1913; Fidelity Trust Com-

Figure 4-1. Artist's depiction of first Europeans arriving on the shores of Newark (Atkinson, 1878).

pany, 1916; Pierson, 1917; Brydon, 1974; Cunningham, 1988) (Figure 4-1).

In 1664 the British acquired the Dutch lands. Lord John Berkeley and Sir George Carteret were the proprietors of English lands in New Jersey. A group of English settlers from New Haven, Connecticut, established Newark in 1666, making it the first official European colony on the Passaic River. Remaining lands along the Passaic were bought and settled over the next half-century. By the time James Wills moved to Roxiticus (in present-day Mendham Township, at the source of the River) in 1717, there were scattered villages and farms at points all along the Passaic (Urquart, 1913; Fidelity Trust Company, 1916; Pierson, 1917; Brydon, 1974; Cunningham, 1988).

Early settlers used the Passaic River and its tributaries for power. Sawmills and gristmills were especially numerous, and their construction was one of the first tasks in each community. Sawmills provided construction lumber and gristmills yielded flour for food and trade. Many of the mills used dams to increase river head and thus, power yield (Brydon, 1974).

Although the early European settlers relied heavily on the Passaic River, through the late 1700s the River's natural character was not greatly impacted (Figure 4-2). However, over the next two centuries the watershed would become a center for commerce and manufacturing, with dramatic effects on the River and its environs.

The Great Falls (at present-day Paterson) symbolized the Passaic's natural values. Poets and artists portrayed the beauty and power of the Falls, and it attracted visitors from near and far (e.g., Macnab, 1890; Williams, 1938). The Godwin House, also

Figure 4-2. Artist's view of Passaic River—late 1700s (from the collections of the Newark Public Library).

known as the Passaic Hotel, was established at the Falls in 1775. Visitors used folios provided by the Godwin house to write about their experience of visiting the Falls, and many carved their initials or names in the face of the cliff. There were so many initials on one part of the rock that it became known as the Grotto of Records. George Washington supposedly carved his initials on the cliff in 1778 (Brydon, 1974).

If the Falls were the River's highlight, they were also involved in its destruction. The Great Falls was an early focus of human interest in the Passaic River. As the terminus of shad and herring runs, the Falls attracted annual attention from the Lenape, who harvested the fish gathered in the downstream pools. Indeed, shad and sturgeon were fished at the Falls until the Dundee Dam was constructed in 1858, ending fish access to the upriver areas.

The Society for Establishing Useful Manufactures (SUM) was organized by Governor Paterson and chartered in November 1791, directing Secretary of the Treasury, Alexander Hamilton, and others to raise capital for establishing a system of "domestic manufactures." Their primary aim was to produce cotton goods. Among other things, the charter authorized the SUM to improve navigation by constructing canals, lakes, and dams. It was up to the SUM to determine where to locate their operations (Cunningham, 1954; Brydon, 1974).

The SUM chose the Great Falls over five other sites for the location of its first factory (Brydon, 1974). Alexander Hamilton had previously employed engineers to test the water of various rivers for purity, and water from the Pequannock—which flows into the Passaic—was the "purest and softest" (Urquhart, 1913). Other factors favoring the selection of the Great Falls included the available power, nearby timber, excellent quarries, ease of navigational improvement, and regional deposits of bog iron ore and red ochre (Brydon, 1974). To repay the Governor's charter, the SUM directors named their developing river town "Paterson" (Brydon, 1974).

The SUM constructed a dam and raceway to divert water from the Falls to the planned factories. A cotton mill was built in 1793 and other sites were leased starting around 1804. Lessees built more mills, in a cascade of industrial growth. Paterson boomed during the War of 1812 because of heavy cotton demand. Industrial activity continued to grow throughout the 19th century (Urquart, 1913; Pierson, 1917; Brydon, 1974; Cunningham, 1988).

Despite the lost visual grandeur, people continued recreational visits to the Falls. July 4th fireworks were held annually starting in 1829, and the celebrations regularly featured balloon ascensions and tightrope walkers. Writers and painters depicted the Falls as late as 1870 (Cawley and Cawley, 1942; Brydon, 1974). Still, the impact of SUM development on the Falls was dramatic. Figures 4-3 and 4-4 show the Great Falls before and after SUM facilities were built on the site.

Industrialization increased along the Passaic River following the SUM's success. Newark, which was primarily a farming community throughout the 1700s, saw its population jump following the construction of two bridges, one over the Hackensack and one over the Passaic. Newark grew from 8,000 inhabitants in 1826 to 18,000 in 1835, a 125% increase in less than a decade. There were 141 dwellings in Newark in 1777; by 1832, there were 1,542 (Urquhart, 1913) (Figures 4-5 and 4-6).

Newark's manufacturing increased enormously from 1790 to 1850. Shoemaking was by far the most common occupation,

Figure 4-3. Artist's view of Great Falls—early 1800s (from the collections of the New Jersey Historical Society).

with 685 shoemakers, followed by production of carriages, with 210 workers (Urquhart, 1913). There were three iron and brass foundries, among other industries (Urquhart, 1913).

Shoes made Newark famous. Moses Combs, the founder of Newark's shoe industry, seized the opportunity to sell shoes *outside* of Newark. From c. 1790 to 1803, Combs' shop supported all Newark's leather business, which included tanning, patterning, cutting, and currying, in addition to shoemaking proper. Around 1803 this industry became more specialized, and separate shops began to carry out each aspect of the leather trade. By 1806, one-third of Newark's inhabitants were engaged in shoe-

Figure 4-4. Artist's view of Great Falls—mid-1800s, following early industrial development (from the collections of the Newark Public Library).

Figure 4-5. City of Newark—1790 (Leary, 1891).

Figure 4-6. City of Newark—mid-1800s (from the collections of the Newark Public Library).

making, according to the caption on an 1806 map made by Charles Basham of the Newark Academy. The War of 1812 created heavy demand for shoes and other leather products, and Newark shipped leather goods to Philadelphia for the military (Urquhart, 1913).

Carriage making was also a successful export industry. Robert B. Campfield became famous for making heavy coaches in the early 1800s. General Santa Anna of Mexico and a leading official in Cuba were two of his most distinguished customers (Urquhart, 1913).

The construction of the Dundee Dam in 1858 at Passaic, between Newark and Paterson, was probably the most significant event related to the industrialization of the Passaic River before the Civil War. This dam, which still stands, followed failed attempts in the 1820s and 1830s to dam the River at this point. Locks were constructed, canals were cut, and mill sites were laid out after the dam was finished. However, there was little traffic through the locks, and the mill sites did not prosper until the 1880s, when the Passaic River basin experienced even more rapid residential and industrial growth (Brydon, 1974; Cunningham, 1988).

The Dundee Dam had mixed effects on recreation. The lake created by the dam was popular with skaters, boaters, and fishermen for many years, until pollution devastated the River in later decades. However, the dam ended the migratory runs of shad and sturgeon, which had been particularly popular with fishermen upriver at the Great Falls in Paterson (Brydon, 1974).

Around the time of the Civil War, the Passaic River supported numerous recreation activities including boating, rowing, fishing, ice skating, and swimming (Figures 4-7 and 4-8). The River was the center of social life for local residents, and its rowing regattas were popular events attended by thousands of people (The Board of Education . . . , 1914; Newark Athletic Club News, 1921; Star-Ledger, 1929; Michelson, 1932; Williams, 1938; Wildes, 1943; Falzer, 1947; White, 1953; McFadden, 1962; Galishoff, 1970):

"In this [the rowing regattas] and in countless other ways, the river afforded an opportunity to escape, if only briefly, from the pressure and discomforts of urban living, and to look upon and delight in nature's wonders." (Galishoff, 1970)

Between 1880 and 1890, urbanization, industrialization, and pollution began to limit recreation opportunities on the River

Figure 4-7. Winter recreation on the Passaic River—1852 (Painting by Edward Beyer, photo reproduction used with permission from the Newark Public Library).

(The Board of Education . . . , 1914; Newark Athletic Club News, 1921; Newark News, 1956; Galishoff, 1970; Brydon, 1974; Cawley and Cawley, 1942). Examples of some of the many industries located along the River by the end of the 19th century and in the beginning of the 20th century are depicted in Figures 4-9 through 4-14. By the 1890s:

> "The fishing industry died and the stately homes and estates along the river were converted into junkyards and smoke-belching factories. Manufacturers utilized the river as a convenient receptacle for industrial wastes. The shortsightedness of this cavalier disregard for a natural resource became apparent during periods of hot weather, when the river emitted a stench so overpowering that factories were forced to stop production. Floating debris, murky water, and raw sewage made swimming unsafe, and the bathhouses on the river had to close. The pleasure craft that had dotted the river were replaced by decaying boat hulks . . ." (Galishoff, 1970)

VOL. XVII.   All the News. Four Editions Daily.   NEW YORK, THURSDAY, AUGUST 22, 1878. $12 Per Year in Advance. Single Copies, Five Cents.   NO. 1691.

THE SIXTH ANNUAL REGATTA OF THE NATIONAL ASSOCIATION OF AMATEUR OARSMEN AT NEWARK. N

Figure 4-8.   Summer recreation on the Passaic River—1878 (from the collections of the Newark Public Library).

Figure 4-9. Blue Stone Company on the Passaic River—Late 1800s (Leary, 1891).

By 1900, sewage and industrial pollution had all but eliminated recreation activities on the Passaic River (Hine, 1909; Newark Athletic Club News, 1921; Star-Ledger, 1929; Star-Ledger, 1946; White, 1953; Newark News, 1956; McFadden, 1962; Galishoff, 1970; Brydon, 1974).

Following the severe environmental decline of the late 1800s, there were many attempts to restore the River and revive recreation (Star-Ledger, 1929; Star-Ledger, 1946; Newark News, 1948; McFadden, 1962; Brydon, 1974). Between 1925 and 1940, conditions improved. A trunk sewer completed in 1924 bypassed the Passaic and carried sewage from municipalities along the River directly into New York Harbor. In the 1930s, the Great Depression limited industrial activity and stabilized population growth. The reduced environmental pressure briefly im-

Figure 4-10. Shipyard on the Passaic River—late 1800s (Leary, 1891).

Figure 4-11. Newark Gas and Light Company on the Passaic River—late 1800s (Leary, 1891).

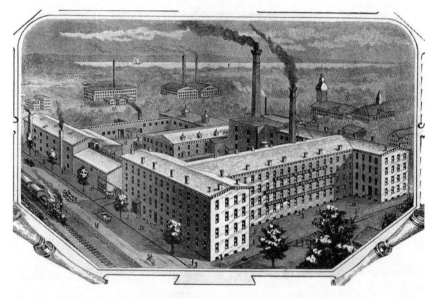

Figure 4-12. Leather goods manufacturing facility on the Passaic River—late 1800s (Leary, 1891).

proved the quality of the River's recreation services (Brydon, 1974; Passaic River Coalition, 1983; Peet and Johnson, 1996).

The environmental recovery was temporary. Industrial activity along the River grew rapidly during World War II. When the United States' economy expanded in the postwar decades, urbanization, industrialization, and pollution pressures again impacted recreation. In 1970 the Passaic River was called the "second most polluted river in the United States" (Peet and Johnson, 1996).

Since the mid-1970s, the quality of recreation services has noticeably improved (Passaic River Coalition, 1983; Peet and Johnson, 1996). Banks are cleaner, some fish species have returned, and debris and abandoned boat hulls are less obvious (Passaic River Coalition, 1983; Crawford *et al.*, 1994; Peet and

Figure 4-13. Newark smelting and refining works—1920 (from the collections of the New Jersey Historical Society).

Figure 4-14. Industry along Passaic River in Newark—mid-1920s (from the collections of the Newark Public Library).

Johnson, 1996). Federal and state pollution-control legislation and the efforts of local community-action groups are largely responsible for this improvement. Opportunities for boating, rowing, and fishing have improved to varying degrees (Metro Newark, 1981; Crawford *et al.*, 1994; Pflugh, 1996).

The discovery of polychlorinated biphenyls (PCBs) in 1978 and dioxin in 1983 raised concerns about sediment and water quality of the Passaic River. The presence of these contaminants led the New Jersey Department of Environmental Protection (NJDEP) to issue fish-consumption advisories in the 1980s, and in 1994, the United States Environmental Protection Agency (USEPA) posted trilingual fishing-advisory signs along the banks of the Passaic River in response to public concern (USEPA, 1994). In recent years a 6-mile reach of the Passaic River, known as the Passaic River Study Area, has been the subject of environmental investigations under Superfund due to the magnitude of historical and present day pollution in this stretch of the River (USEPA, 1999).

European settlement had dramatic impacts on the Passaic River and its ecosystems. The available records show the degradation beginning as early as the end of the 18th century when European settlers founded the Society for Establishing Useful Manufactures, thus initiating the long history of trading off environmental quality for economic development. The linked events of industrialization and urbanization effectively destroyed the Passaic's ecosystems by the early part of the 20th century. The following chapters describe in more detail the impacts of these events on the River over time.

5

SHORELINES AND WETLANDS
What Happened to Them?

*"Where there is a large population and little land,
the land automatically becomes very valuable."*

J. Teal and M. Teal (1969)

THROUGHOUT THE 19ᵀᴴ AND 20ᵀᴴ centuries, urbanization and industrial development dramatically altered the shorelines of the Passaic River. Piers and docks were built in the River. Bulkheads were constructed. The shores were rip-rapped with rock and construction debris (Squires and Barclay, 1990). Development narrowed the width of the Passaic River by nearly one-half in some reaches. The environmental effects were substantial. In particular, the River has lost nearly all of its nearshore riparian habitats (aquatic and wetland ecosystems).

The loss of shorelines and wetlands likely represents the single most devastating and permanent impact to the ecology of the Passaic River and Newark Bay. Fish, shellfish, birds, mammals, and other animals depend heavily on wetlands and nearshore habitats for food, cover, and breeding. This is particularly true for estuaries, where marshes, submerged aquatic vegetation (SAV) beds, and tidal creeks are typically the most important habitats and are responsible for much of the primary and secondary production that occurs within the ecosystem (Teal and Teal, 1969; Festa and Toth, 1976; Pomeroy and Wiegert, 1981; Day *et al.*, 1989; Mitsch and Gosselink, 1993; Vernburg, 1993). The loss of these habitats not only affects the ecology of the River itself, but limits the use of the Estuary by migratory animals, thus affecting production of ecologically and economically important species. Although the estuarine portion of the Passaic River is small compared to other rivers on the east coast, the incremental wetlands and shoreline losses are important, since similar impacts have occurred in many other east coast estuaries. The overall cumulative impact of these incremental losses is large. More than 50% of the pre-Columbian wetlands that once existed on the east coast of the U.S. have been lost to human development (Dahl *et al.*, 1990; Mitsch and Gosselink, 1993).

This chapter details historical shoreline development of the Passaic River, Newark Bay, and the lower Hackensack River. Collectively, these wetlands and waterways were once an integrated and productive landscape. Today, the wetland and shoreline losses are reflected in a depauperate and impoverished ecology.

Wetlands

Before European colonization, the tidal portion of the Passaic River, the Hackensack River, and Newark Bay supported extensive tidal and freshwater marshes (Figure 5-1), which ran far upstream. The "Newark Meadows" near Elizabeth was an area of

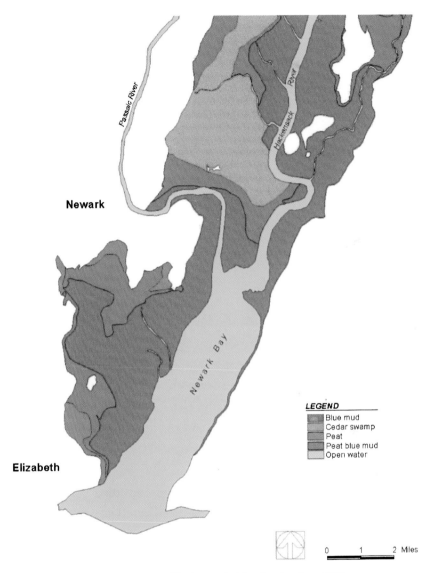

Figure 5-1. Wetlands of the Hackensack Meadowlands—1870.

more than 7,000 acres of tidal marsh. Marshes of the lower Passaic and Hackensack Rivers (together called the Hackensack Meadowlands) had an area of more than 20,000 acres, 1,465 of which were tidal freshwater. About one-third of the area of the Hackensack Meadowlands was covered by white cedar swamp (Jenkinson, 1912; Heusser, 1963; Squires, 1981; Kraus and Smith, 1988; Squires and Barclay, 1990; Berger, 1992; Squires, 1992).

Lands around the Passaic River and Newark Bay were altered as soon as Europeans arrived in the 17th century. Robert Treat and John Gregory surveyed the Passaic River in 1655. During their voyage, they observed that "salt marsh marked both sides of the lower valley as far as the eye could see" and that "tall salt grass fringed the right bank well past the River's second great meander." By the late 1660s, the Passaic River Valley was changing with homes being built along the waterways, meadowlands being burned, and commuting paths defined. During this time, maintenance of public facilities was shared among the settlers. They kept the roadways clear, the meadows ditched, fences repaired, woods burned, and common lands open to pasture cattle (Jacobson, 1957). Marsh draining, timber harvest, and tidal flow restrictions were all part of this shared maintenance. For many years, the marshes were seen as "a blight upon the surrounding country" (Vermeule, 1896). Early settlers graded hills and filled portions of the wetlands for cultivation (Urquhart, 1913). Drainage ditches and tidal exclusion dikes were built throughout the colonial period, and much of the marshland between Newark and New York was ditched by the late 1700s (Headlee, 1945). When industry expanded, ditching and diking accelerated.

Since 1816, about 88% of the wetlands associated with the lower Passaic River and Newark Bay have been lost (Figures 5-2 through 5-6 and Table 5-1). These wetland areas were ditched, diked, and drained and then later "reclaimed" with as much as 13 feet of fill material on the original marsh surface (Squires, 1992).

Some marshes were diked for salt hay production. Salt hay is grass grown in tidelands from which tidal flow is restricted or eliminated. The wetland soils are highly productive and the hay is abundant and nutritious. European species of grasses were introduced for fodder. Between 1816 and 1819, a 1,300-acre tract of marshland south of Sawmill Creek was diked for gardens and dairies. Over 7 miles of embankments and 120 miles of ditches were built in the marsh (Wright, 1988). Two long drainage ditches, Peddie Ditch and Flushing Ditch, can be seen crossing the Newark Meadows from west to east towards Newark Bay in the 1889 Newark atlas by Scarlett and Scarlett (1889). These ditches undoubtedly dried a large area of wetland, and impacted the ecology in many ways.

Beginning in the 1830s, more wetlands were filled and graded to build railroad beds (Quinn, 1997). When state geologist, C.C. Vermeule, wrote his 1896 report on the drainage of the Hackensack and Newark marshes, the wetlands were criss-crossed by 12 large railway lines, six of which were main trunks. In fact, rail lines crossed the marshes before many of the conventional roadways were built (Quinn, 1997) (Figure 5-7). Cedar trees were cut from the swamps for trestle supports—they were "a cheap and durable lumber" (Quinn, 1997). "Countless tons of dirt" were required to build up the roadbed bases (Cunningham, 1951).

The Dundee Dam across the Passaic River was completed in

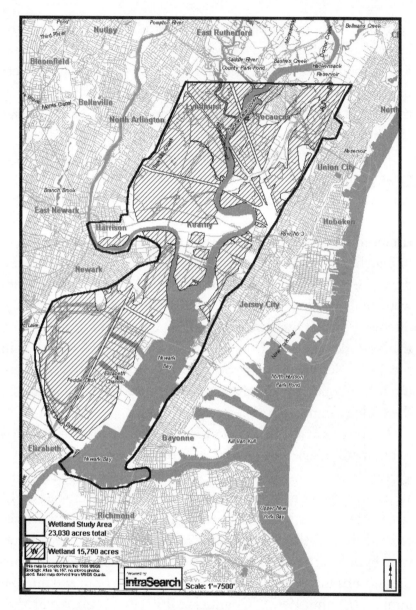

Figure 5-2. Extent of wetlands—1905 (IntraSearch, 1999).

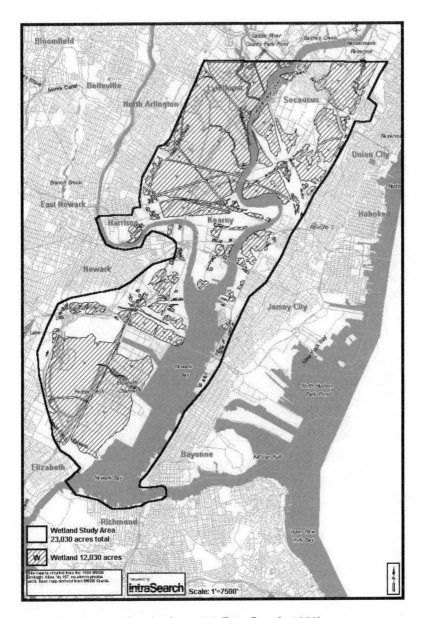

Figure 5-3. Extent of wetlands—1932 (IntraSearch, 1999).

Figure 5-4. Extent of wetlands—1954 (IntraSearch, 1999).

Figure 5-5.   Extent of wetlands—1976 (IntraSearch, 1999).

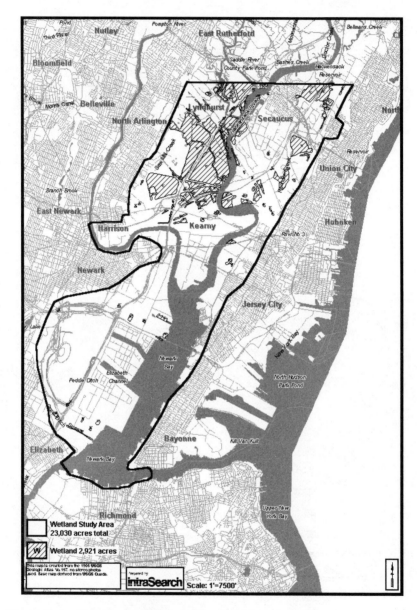

Figure 5-6. Extent of wetlands—1997 (IntraSearch, 1999).

Table 5-1. Estimates of historical wetland losses in the lower Passaic River and Newark Bay region

| Year | Acres of Wetlands | Wetland Losses | | | |
| | | Incremental | | Cumulative | |
		Acres	Percent	Acres	Percent
Pre-1816[a]	24,728	—	—	—	—
1870	18,428	6,300	26	6,300	26
1905	15,356	3,072	17	9,372	38
1932	12,030	3,326	22	12,698	51
1940	11,180	850	7	13,548	55
1954	8,738	2,442	22	15,990	65
1966	5,574	3,164	36	19,154	77
1976	3,570	2,004	36	21,158	86
1989	3,058	512	14	21,670	88
1997	2,921	137	4	21,807	88

Notes:
[a] Based on sum of mapped wetlands in 1870 and reported wetlands losses for period of 1816 through 1867.

1858. Water flow in the River was dramatically decreased. A smaller dam was built just upstream of the Great Falls. During summer low flows and droughts, flow over the falls was "reduced to a mere trickle." At the turn of the century, water diversions had left "bare river bed" in portions of the upstream River (Leighton, 1902). By 1908, low flows due to the dam and to increased use of the waters of the upper Passaic, caused a drop in the daily dry-weather flow from 85 million to about 35 million gallons (Brydon, 1974).

This enormous decrease had important impacts on the ecology and use of the Passaic River. The reduced freshwater flow increased saltwater intrusion and moved the head of the tide upstream. Salinity gradients increased in the lower River. Floral

Figure 5-7.   Map of railroads in the Newark region—1887 (Van Cleef and Betts, 1887).

surveys conducted in the lower reaches of the Hackensack and Passaic Rivers by John Torrey (1819) and published as a *Catalogue of Plants, Growing Spontaneously Within Thirty Miles of the City of New York* identified more than 190 species, none of which were salt tolerant. By 1889, Britton catalogued 22 species of plants in the area, seven of which were salt tolerant. The Oradell Dam, built in 1921, cut off much of the freshwater flow to the lower Hackensack and moved its head of the tide upstream. As the population served by the Oradell Reservoir grew, freshwater flows decreased even more. The resulting higher salinity environment altered wetlands and impacted biodiversity. Plant and animal communities in the lower Passaic and Hackensack Rivers changed as the environment shifted from freshwater to brackish water (Sipple, 1972; Russell, 1980; Rogers and Rowntree, 1988).

The shoreline alterations of the 19th and 20th centuries dramatically affected Newark Bay as well. In the late 1800s and early 1900s, wetlands in the southern Hackensack were filled to create land for oil storage and refining facilities (Squires, 1992). Industrial activity expanded when the United States entered World War I, and marshes in Kearny and Newark were converted to shipbuilding ports (Cunningham, 1966; 1994). Between 1914 and 1915, a port channel 1 mile long, 100 yards wide, and 7 yards deep was dug across the Newark Meadows from Newark Bay to Peddie Ditch. At this time, one-third of the city was still considered "swampland," but the wetland area was shrinking rapidly (Cunningham, 1988). In 1917, 28 wharves were built at Port Newark for the first shipyard of the Submarine Boat Company. The first ship launched was called the Agawam, which is the Lenape word for "Great Salt Meadow" (Cummings, 1998a).

Figure 5-8. Mosquito ditching activities in the Hackensack Meadowlands—1930s (Headlee, 1945; with permission from Rutgers University Press).

Another surge of wetland drainage began in the early 1900s when ditching was increased for mosquito control (Figure 5-8). Attempts to control mosquitoes were underway as early as the late 1660s, but increased greatly as the population grew. In the early 1900s, New Jersey was infested with mosquitoes. Mosquito control was seen as a viable option, both for eliminating the insects and converting "wasted" wetlands into productive fastland. According to Headlee and Carroll (1919), a crucial step in promoting industrial development was draining the wetlands and eliminating mosquito breeding grounds. Getting rid of wetlands, "where workmen are tormented throughout the summer season by hordes of winged pests," was seen as a key to increasing development (Headlee and Carroll, 1919). In addition to ditching, marshes were filled for the complete elimination of mosquito breeding ground. Sod from the ditches was used to fill small pools of water and killifish were added to larger pools to consume mosquito larvae (Headlee, 1945). Mosquito breeding within the ditches themselves was temporarily controlled by applications of oil or larvicidal chemicals to the water in the ditch (Headlee, 1935).

On May 19, 1904, the Legislature of the Conference Committee on Mosquito Extermination passed an anti-mosquito clause that was part of the New Jersey General Health Act. The organization was renamed the North Jersey Mosquito Extermination League in 1910 and had representatives from Newark, New Brunswick, Orange, Harrison, Springfield, Summit, Bloomfield, Arlington, Kearny, South Orange, Irvington, Montclair, Belleville, West Orange, Glen Ridge, Plainfield, and Elizabeth (Headlee, 1945). Counties bordering the marshes formed their own Mosquito Extermination Commissions. The commissions began work in Essex and Union counties in 1912 (Headlee and Carroll, 1919) and within 3 years had expanded into Hudson, Passaic, and Bergen counties.

By 1914, the Hudson County Mosquito Extermination Commission completed extensive ditching along Frank's Creek, one of the few small tributaries that still flows today into the lower Passaic. "By 1924, the Bergen County Mosquito Commission alone had a million feet of drainage ditches on the salt marsh and over 500,000 feet of upland ditches under its jurisdiction" (Headlee, 1945). Beginning in 1906, the New Jersey Agricultural Experiment Station installed as many salt-marsh drainage systems as funding would allow. By 1945, "Much, but not all, of the salt marsh along the Hackensack River and Newark Bay, approximately 26,000 acres [had] been ditched and diked, and the remainder [had] been ditched." (Headlee, 1945). In the 1930s, large tracts of these drained salt marshes were overrun by dense stands of cattails (*Typha* species) and common reed (*Phragmites australis*) (Urner, 1935; Wright, 1988).

Throughout the 19th and 20th centuries the areas of the Hackensack Meadowlands not diked, drained, or filled were used as dumping grounds for municipal and industrial wastes (Figure 5-9). Unregulated dumping converted many acres of wetlands into uplands. Unregulated dumps were closed in the 1970s, but today there are more than 2,500 acres of refuse-filled marsh (Brydon, 1974; Sullivan, 1998).

Construction of the Newark International Airport began in 1928. Dredged material from Newark Bay was piped into the Hackensack Meadowlands for fill. More than 915,500 cubic yards of dry fill were added to bring the land up to grade (Cunningham, 1988). Originally, 68 acres of marsh were set aside and filled for the building of the airport. Both the port and the airport expanded after World War II. Today, the airport occupies nearly 2,500 acres of reclaimed wetlands (USEPA/USACE, 1995).

The loss of wetlands along the lower Passaic River increased dramatically following the war. The U.S. Army Corps of Engi-

Figure 5-9. Garbage disposal in the Hackensack Meadowlands (Headlee, 1945; with permission from Rutgers University Press).

neers (USACE) estimates that between 1940 and 1978, more than 7,500 acres of wetlands were filled and developed in the Lower Passaic Valley (USACE, 1987). Then, after hundreds of years and thousands of acres of wetlands destruction, the state of New Jersey legislature passed the Coastal Wetlands Protection Act in 1970 with the goal of preserving the state's remaining coastal wetlands. In spite of this and other regulations passed in subsequent years, wetland reclamation appears to have continued after 1970. For instance, according to the USACE (1987) more than 1,200 acres of wetlands along the Passaic River were lost between 1978 and 1984. More than 500 acres of wetlands were apparently being actively filled as late as 1987 (USEPA/ USACE, 1995).

As of the mid-1980s, only a few "pockets" of wetlands remained along the lower Passaic River. Today, less than 1% of the original wetlands remain in the Passaic River near its confluence with Newark Bay (Peet and Johnson, 1996). According to the Passaic River Coalition, only 84 of an estimated 7,400 acres of original wetlands remain in the lower Passaic Valley (Peet and Johnson, 1996).

Tributaries

Many tributaries once flowed to the lower Passaic River and Newark Bay (Figure 5-10). More than 78 miles of tributaries to the lower Passaic River and Newark Bay were converted into storm sewer drains or filled by 1950 (Table 5-2).

Great Meadow Brook was a substantial tributary to Second River. The confluence of the two rivers was located just east of Hendrick Mills, probably near what is now known as Hendricks Pond (Folsom, 1900; Rankin, 1930). Great Meadow Brook and two of its larger tributaries were drawn on the 1896 topographical map by Vermeule and an 1899 Geological Survey of New Jersey, but none of them were named. The watershed included parts of East Orange, Bloomfield, Belleville, and Newark.

Two other small, unnamed brooks entered the Passaic River near First River, one to the north and one to the south. These brooks were described by Rankin (1930) and Urquhart (1913) and are depicted on historical maps (e.g., Strims, 1795; Stone, 1839; Pierce *et al.*, 1874). Many small brooks drained the marshes and entered the lower Passaic just south of Newark, in

ID	Waterway	Information Sources Maps	Literature
A	Great Meadow Brook	Leffingwell, 1865; Cook & Vermeule, 1890; Geological Survey, 1899	Rankin, 1927; Rankin, 1930
B	Great Meadow Brook Tributary through Boiling Springs	Leffingwell, 1865; Cook & Vermeule, 1890; Geological Survey, 1899	Rankin, 1927
C	Great Meadow Brook Tributary	Leffingwell, 1865; Cook & Vermeule, 1890; Geological Survey, 1899	
D	Branch Brook	Van Winkle, 1847	Urquhart, 1913; Rankin, 1930
E	First River (Mill Brook)	Van Winkle, 1847; Van Duyne & Sherman, 1868; Cook & Vermeule, 1890	Urquhart, 1913; Rankin, 1930
F	First River Tributaries	Van Winkle, 1847	
G	Unnamed Creeks		Urquhart, 1913; Rankin, 1930; Rankin, 1927
H	Bound Creek (Wequahic Creek)	Van Winkle, 1847; Kummel, 1908; Rankin, 1918; NJDEP, 1982	
I	Two-Mile Creek	Van Winkle, 1847	Rankin, 1930; Urquhart, 1913; Rankin, 1930
J	Hayes Brook	Van Winkle, 1847	Urquhart, 1913; Rankin, 1930
K	Wheeler's Creek	Van Winkle, 1847; Kummel, 1908; Rankin, 1918; NJDEP, 1982	
L	Maple Island Creek	Kummel, 1908; NJDEP, 1982	
M	Dead Creek (Club Creek)	Kummel, 1908; NJDEP, 1982	
N	Pierson Creek	Kummel, 1908; NJDEP, 1982	
O	Jaspers Creek	Kummel, 1908; NJDEP, 1982	
P	Morris Creek	Kummel, 1908; NJDEP, 1982	
Q	Fishing Creek	Kummel, 1908; NJDEP, 1982	
R	Stoffel Creek	Kummel, 1908; NJDEP, 1982	
S	Oyster Creek	Kummel, 1908; NJDEP, 1982	
T	Sloping Creek	Kummel, 1908; NJDEP, 1982	
U	Forked Creek	Kummel, 1908; NJDEP, 1982	
V	Woodruff's Creek	Kummel, 1908; NJDEP, 1982	
	Kearny Marsh Tributaries	Pierce et al., 1874; Kummel, 1908	
	Upper Newark Bay Tributaries	Pierce et al., 1874; Rankin, 1918; NJDEP, various dates	

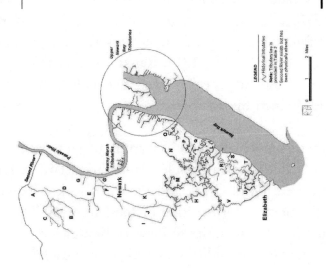

Figure 5-10. Historical rivers, creeks, and tributaries of the lower Passaic River and Newark Bay

Table 5-2. Estimated losses of historical rivers, creeks, and tributaries in the lower Passaic River and Newark Bay

River/Creek	Estimated Length Lost (mi)
Bound Creek and Tributaries	18.1
Maple Island Creek and Tributaries	13.2
First River and Tributaries	6.0
Unnamed Passaic Tributary Creeks	0.7
Kearny Marsh Tributaries	1.2
Great Meadow Brook and Tributaries	6.3
Oyster Creek and Tributaries	2.3
Upper Newark Bay Tributaries	10.9
Other Newark Bay Tributaries	20.2
Total Lost	78.9

Harrison and near Point No Point. Several historical maps show the former locations of these brooks (Pierce *et al.*, 1874; Kummel, 1908; Board of Public Improvements . . . , 1997).

An extensive network of creeks meandered through the Newark Meadows, draining the marshes into Newark Bay (Figure 5-10). The largest of these was Bound Creek. Bound Creek originated in Wequahic Lake and was sometimes called Wequahic Creek (Rankin, 1918; Rankin, 1927). Three lengthy tributaries of Bound Creek flowed generally from north to south and drained the southwestern part of the current city of Newark.

Another major tributary to Newark Bay that flowed through the Newark Meadows was Maple Island Creek. Two of its larger tributaries were Dead Creek and Pierson Creek. These creeks drained the northeastern section of the Meadows. There were numerous smaller tributaries to Newark Bay, including Fishing Creek, Jasper's Creek, and Plum Creek, to name a few.

The losses of a few of the Passaic River tributaries are well documented with dates and descriptions of the activities leading to the losses (Urquhart, 1913; Rankin, 1927; Rankin, 1930). The meandering Wheeler's Creek tributary was evidently straightened into a ditch, and the ditch was named after the Creek (Van Winkle, 1847). Accounts of the causes of loss for First River (Mill Brook), Great Meadow Brook, and Boiling Springs, which were all tributaries of the Passaic River, are described below. Others, such as Hayes Brook, simply disappeared over time, unaccounted, from the maps of the region. Apparently, the tributaries to Newark Bay that drained the Newark Meadows and the small tributaries to the Passaic River in the Kearny marshes were lost when the marshes were filled.

The largest and arguably the most important Passaic River tributary that was lost was First River (Mill Brook) (Cook and Vermeule, 1890; Urquhart, 1913; Rankin, 1930). Maps of Newark from 1668 and 1795 show First River as the northern boundary of the city, entering the Passaic at what is now the Clay Street Bridge (Strims, 1795; Van Winkle, 1847; Cook and Vermeule, 1890; Brydon, 1974). First River was used as a source of power for gristmills and as a public water supply for the early city. The River began to disappear in 1863 when it had outlived its usefulness to the city. Sections of First River were filled over the next 27 years. In 1890, the last piece was covered by the approach to the Clay Street Bridge (Rankin, 1930). The only trace of the old river remaining on present-day maps are the lakes in Branch Brook Park that were formed by portions of the Branch Brook tributary to First River.

Great Meadow Brook was a tributary of Second River. The Great Meadow Brook watershed was about 1,500 acres. A small dam on the Brook created Silver Lake. The dam was washed out by a storm in 1889, and Silver Lake disappeared. The lakebed was later filled and replaced with streets and houses. Subsequently, the Great Meadow Brook was converted into a narrow, zigzag ditch intended to handle storm runoff. South of Bloomfield Avenue, the Brook and one of its branches were replaced with covered storm-water sewers (Rankin, 1930). According to Rankin (1930), the municipalities of East Orange, Belleville, and Bloomfield entered into an agreement to replace the remainder of the Brook with storm-water sewers by 1931. One of the branches of Great Meadow Brook passed through Boiling Springs, once a public water supply. In 1910, "the East Orange and Ampere Land Company, in developing their tracts, drained off the water [of Boiling Springs] through an underground conduit," and no trace of the spring remained (Rankin, 1918).

The 1908 geological survey map by H.B. Kummel, based on a 1905 survey, shows that many of the Newark Bay tributaries were still in existence. Only a few of these, Bound and Maple Island creeks and a few smaller tributaries, are shown 10 years later on Rankin's (1918) historical map. By 1950, all the tributaries depicted in Figure 5-10 were gone, due to marsh reclamation in the Newark Meadows during the first half of the 20th century.

Riverbanks

The Passaic River was narrowed considerably when shorelines were expanded by placing fill into the River to create additional land for industrial sites. In some locations, the River was narrowed by as much as one-half (NJDEP, 1972–1980) (Figure 5-11). Below Second River, across the stream from the Mount Pleasant Cemetery, there was once a small sedge-covered island

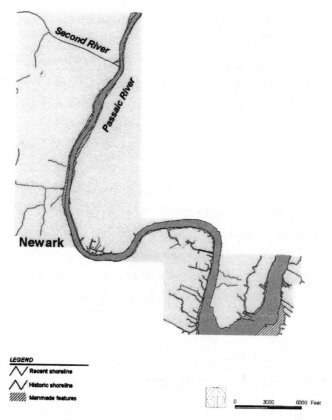

Figure 5-11. Lower Passaic River shoreline changes

known as Green Island that was "a noted rendezvous for wild ducks and geese" (Hine, 1909). A channel about 50 yards wide separated the island from the western bank of the Passaic (Rankin, 1930). The Island was described as a "hunter's paradise," and shad and smelt were caught in the narrow channel (Hine, 1909). In the mid-1800s, the channel between Green Island and the west bank of the Passaic was completely filled to become the bed of the Paterson Branch of the Erie Railroad. The

71

eastern shore of Green Island was extended by fill placed into the River (Rankin, 1930).

Much of the fill material used to reclaim Passaic River wetlands for commercial and residential development was dredged from the River's shipping channel. In 1896, C.C. Vermeule wrote in the *Annual Report of the State Geologist*:

> *"We have considered three methods of reclaiming these lands, which have been suggested at different times. The first is filling-in by dredging open canals through the marsh, the dredged material to be used in raising the intervening lands above the level of high water . . . Such a treatment would be suitable along the banks of the Passaic and Hackensack, where material could be obtained either by widening the river channels and deepening them, or by dredging basins and slips."*

Riverbank bulkheads reduced dredged material disposal costs. A 1922 USACE report states:

> *"If proper bulkheads or dikes be constructed along these bulkhead lines, and if the space shoreward of these lines be used for spoil areas [for the dredged materials], the cost of the dredging would be moderate, and the benefit to owners in the way of reclaimed lands would be large."*

Both the riverbank bulkheading, and the wetland reclamation drastically altered the natural, land-shore interface of the Passaic River. It was certainly conducive to commerce. But the economic advantages were obtained at a substantial cost to the environment.

Two USACE reports (1912 and 1922) indicate the extent of the shoreline alteration at different periods. In 1910 there were 128 wharves on the Passaic River between Newark and the town of Passaic. Eleven wharves were open for public access (USACE, 1912). The remainder were held privately by commercial enterprises or individuals.

Table 5-3 documents the extent of shoreline modification along the Passaic River's banks by 1922. The total number of structures includes docks, wharves, and riverbank bulkhead both below and above the Montclair and Greenwood Lake Railroad Bridge, eight miles upstream from the mouth of the Passaic River (see Figure 1-1). Below the bridge, 39% (6.2 out of 16 miles) of the River's shoreline was occupied by docks, wharves, and bulkhead. Between this bridge and the W. Eighth St. Bridge in Passaic, 8% (1.1 out of 14.6 miles) of the shoreline was devoted to docks, wharves, and bulkhead.

Shoreline development increased throughout the 20th century. Figure 5-12 shows the percent of developed versus undeveloped shoreline from 1922 to 1998. In 1922, 24% of the shoreline was developed. In 1998, 86% of the shoreline was de-

Table 5-3. Number and length of structures built on the shorelines of the lower Passaic River by 1922

	Lower 8.0 Miles	Next 7.3 Miles	Total
Number of structures	95	32	127
Linear feet of structures	32,505	6,025	38,530
Miles of structures	6.2	1.1	7.3
Percentage of River Miles	39%	8%	24%

Source: USACE, 1922.

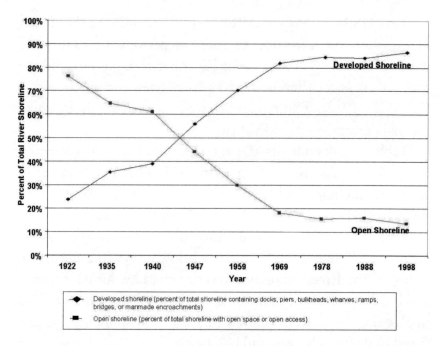

Figure 5-12. Percent shoreline development in the lower Passaic River, 1922–1998

veloped. As Figure 5-12 indicates, shoreline development increased sharply from 1922 to 1969. Shoreline development has increased little from 1969 to now, largely because little undeveloped area remains.

6

WATERWAYS
How Have They Changed
in 300 Years?

*"Newark Bay is an armpit of New York Harbor,
a geographical relationship fully consistent with its popular image."*

J. Waldman (1999)

THE LOWER PASSAIC RIVER, Newark Bay, and their tributaries have been heavily impacted by industrial and municipal development since the 1700s. The Newark metropolitan area has been one of the largest manufacturing centers in the eastern United States since the mid-19th century (Cunningham, 1988; Galishoff, 1988; USEPA/USACE, 1995). For more than 150 years, development along the Passaic River has been spurred by extensive dredging, massive bridge construction, and heavy commercial shipping. Waste disposal, atmospheric deposition, and accidental spills have contaminated the Passaic's water and sediments with sewage and toxic chemicals. Over time, the Passaic was transformed from a recreational to a strictly commercial resource.

Dredging

Beginning in 1874, Newark Bay and the Passaic River were frequently dredged to deepen channels for commercial ships. A 1922 USACE report on the Passaic River states:

> *"The improvement now desired is such enlargement of these channels as will permit ocean-going vessels to engage in traffic with Port Newark Terminal and with existing and proposed industrial developments on these waters. The commerce of the locality is growing and the adjacent territory is rapidly developing . . . There is now an urgent demand for a sufficient depth to accommodate ocean-going vessels not only at the terminals just referred to but at various industrial plants located or proposed on adjacent waters."*

Table 6-1 summarizes dredging activity on the Passaic River between 1874 and 1983. Since 1874, the USACE has dredged more than 20 million cubic yards of sediment from the Passaic River. Dredging deepened portions of Newark Bay and the Passaic to as much as 30 feet.

Bridges

Bridge construction has greatly impacted the recreational quality of the Passaic River by impairing boat passage. The first bridge was built in Paterson before 1737 (Brydon, 1974). Many bridges were built and destroyed throughout the 18th and 19th centuries. When in place, they interfered with recreational navigation.

Table 6-1.   Summary of historical dredging activities in the Passaic River

Date	Location	Approximate River Reach (Miles)	Depth of Dredging (Feet)	Volume of Dredged Material (Cubic Yards)
1874[a]	Belleville Bar	8.0–8.4	7.5	Over 16,400
1874[a]	Rutherford Park Bar	11.9–12.4	6	[b]
1876[a]	Holsman's Bar	12.4–12.6	6	[b]
1876[a]	Small bar above Holsman's Bar	12.6	[b]	[b]
1878[a]	Shoal removed near Erie Railway Bridge at Passaic	13.6	[b]	[b]
1879[a]	Widened channels through all bars from Holsman's Bar to Erie Railway Bridge at Passaic	12.6–13.6	[b]	[b]
1883	Newark to Midland RR bridge	6.0–8.0	6	19,200
1884[a]	Mouth of Passaic to Pennsylvania RR bridge at Center St.	0.0–5.4	10	165,300
1899	Plank Road to Center Street Bridge	1.9–5.4	10	27,600
1899[a]	Widen channel at Rutherford Park Bar	11.9–12.4	[b]	[b]
1899[a]	Remove boulders between Belleville and Passaic	9.0–13.2	[b]	[b]
1906[a]	Newark Bay to Nairn Linoleum Works[c]	Bay–6.5	12	[b]
1906[a]	Nairn Linoleum Works to Montclair & Greenwood Lake RR Bridge[c]	6.5–8.0	10	[b]
1913[a]	Newark Bay to Delaware, Lackawanna & Western RR bridge	Bay–5.8	16	3,153,600
1914[a]	Newark Bay to Pennsylvania RR Freight Bridge at Point-No-Point	Bay–1.9	20–22	2,245,800
1915[a]	Montclair & Greenwood Lake RR bridge to city of Passaic	8.0–13.2	6 to 7	16,500
1916[a]	Newark Bay to Montclair & Greenwood Lake RR Bridge	Bay–8.0	16–17	1,328,300
1916	Pennsylvania RR Freight Bridge at Point-No-Point to 800 feet below Jackson Street	2.6–4.5	20–21	685,000
1917	Newark Bay to a point 2,000 feet above Plank Road Bridge	Bay–2.0	21–22	985,400
1919	Jackson St., Newark to Clay St., Newark	4.6–6.4	16	185,200
1921	Junction to Jackson St., Newark	0.0–4.6	20	102,700
1922	Vicinity of CRR of NJ Bridge to Jackson St., Newark Area	1.4–4.2	20	578,300
1923	Vicinity of Jackson St., Newark	4.2–4.6	20	159,200

Table 6-1. (continued)

Date	Location	Approximate River Reach (Miles)	Depth of Dredging (Feet)	Volume of Dredged Material (Cubic Yards)
1927	Belleville	8.0–9.0	6	2,700
1929	Belleville	8.0–9.0	6	3,900
1930	Belleville	8.0–9.0	10	36,700
1931	Vicinity of Second River	8.1–15.4	10	697,100
1932	Junction to 3,000 ft above Lincoln Hwy. Bridge	0.0–2.6	30	1,430,700
1932	Second River to 8th St.	8.1–15.4	10	602,000
1933	Junction to Rt. 95 Bridge, Newark	0.0–2.5	30	607,200
1933	Vicinity Longoleum Mfg. Co. to Erie R.R. Bridge	6.0–6.3	16	228,300
1934	Belleville Bar	8.0–8.4	10	30,000
1937	3,000 ft above Lincoln Hwy. Bridge to Jackson St., Newark	2.6–4.6	20	800,900
1938	Vicinity of Montclair & Greenwood Lake R.R. Bridge	8.0	10	32,600
1939	Mouth of Second River, Belleville, and between Union Ave. Bridge Rutherford & 2nd St. Bridge Passaic	8.1, 13.2–14.7	10	3,200
1940	Mouth of Second River, Belleville, and between Union Ave. Bridge Rutherford & 2nd St. Bridge Passaic	8.1, 13.2–14.7	10	51,800
1941	Junction to Rt. 95 Bridge	0.0–2.5	30	1,202,000
1945	Opposite Second River	8.1	10	25,600
1946	Junction to Center St. Bridge	0.0–2.5	30	934,500
1949	Penn R.R. Freight Bridge	4.9–5.0	16	272,800
1950	Penn R.R. Freight Bridge	4.9–5.0	16	97,100
1950	Center St. Bridge to Nairn Linoleum Works	5.5–7.0	16	344,700
1950	Gregory Avenue Bridge to 8th St. Bridge	14.3–15.4	10	153,500
1951	Junction to Vicinity of Central RR of NJ Bridge	0.0–1.3	30	329,200
1953	Junction to 500 feet north of Junction	0.0–0.1	30	10,000
1956	Vicinity of Second River	8.1	10	37,200
1957	Junction to Vicinity of Glen. Pulaski Skyway	0.0–2.1	30	413,900
1962	Junction to Vicinity of Central RR of NJ Bridge	0.0–1.2	30	245,400
1965	Junction to U.S. Rt.1 and 9 Bridge, Newark	0.0–1.8	30	505,500
1971	Junction to U.S. Rt.1 and 9 Bridge, Newark	0.0–1.5	30	155,600

Table 6-1. (continued)

Date	Location	Approximate River Reach (Miles)	Depth of Dredging (Feet)	Volume of Dredged Material (Cubic Yards)
1972	Junction to U.S. Rt.1 and 9 Bridge, Newark	0.0–1.8	30	174,600
1974	Vicinity of Second River	8.1	10	65,000
1976	Rutgers St., Belleville Vicinity to Riverside Park, Lyndhurst	9.0–10.2	10	191,600
1977	Junction to Vicinity of Central RR of NJ Bridge	0.0–1.2	30	478,000
1983	Junction to U.S. Rt. 1 and 9 Bridge, Newark	0.0–1.9	30	540,000

Notes:
[a] Project spanned more than one year.
[b] Data not available.
[c] Some of this dredging may have been incorporated into later projects.
Sources: USACE, 1880; 1884; 1900; 1907; 1913; 1915; 1916; 1917.

After demolition or destruction by floods, wars, ice and age, they contributed to the River's heavy load of debris (Brydon, 1974). Presently, there are 28 bridges on the Passaic River between Newark Bay and Dundee Dam (Table 6-2).

Commercial Shipping

Increased industry was reflected in the growth of commercial shipping. Figure 6-1 shows the trend in commercial shipping volume in both the Newark Bay Complex and the Passaic River between 1880 and 1997. In both Newark Bay and the Passaic River, there was a steady increase in commercial shipping from 1880 to 1928. Activity increased rapidly following World War II and peaked on the Passaic in 1968 (11.4 million tons). The Newark Bay Complex (i.e., Newark Bay and its tributaries)

Table 6-2. Bridges over the Passaic River from Newark Bay to Dundee Dam

Name	Location (miles above mouth)	Date Constructed	Type	Horizontal Clearance (ft)	Vertical Clearance (ft)[a] (low water)	(high water)
Central Railroad of New Jersey[b]	Newark and Kearny (1.1)	[d]	Lift	100	30	25
Lincoln Hwy Bridge (Routes 1-9)[c]	Newark (1.8)	1943	Lift	300	45 (140)	40 (135)
Pulaski Skyway	Newark (2.0)	1932	Fixed	520	140	135
Point-No-Point Conrail	Newark (2.6)	1901	Swing	103	21	16
NJ Turnpike	Newark & Kearny (2.7)	1970	Fixed	352	105	100
Jackson St. Bridge[c]	Newark (4.6)	1997	Swing	72	20	15
Amtrak's Dock Bridge	Newark & Harrison (5.0)	1939	Lift	200	29 (143)	24 (138)
Pennsylvania Railroad Bridge at Market Street[b]	Newark (5.1)	[d]	Draw	75	3	21
Pennsylvania Railroad Bridge at Center Street[b]	Newark (5.4)	[d]	Draw	80	3	10
Bridge St. Bridge	Newark (5.6)	1913	Swing	80	12	7
Morristown Line Bridge	Harrison (5.8)	1903	Swing	77	20	15
Rt. 280 (Stickle Memorial Bridge)	E. Newark (5.8)	1944	Lift	200	40 (140)	35 (135)
Clay St. Bridge	Newark (6.0)	1908	Swing	75	13	8
Fourth Ave. Bridge–Conrail	Newark (6.3)	1922	Bascule	126	12	7
Montclair and Greenwood Lake Railroad Bridge[c]	Newark & W. Arlington (8.0)	1937	Swing	48	40	35
Rt. 7 (Rutgers St.) Bridge[c]	Belleville (8.9)	1936	Bascule	98	13	8
Avondale Bridge (DeJessa Memorial)	Avondale (10.7)	1905	Swing	65	12	7
Conrail-Boonton Branch	Lyndhurst (11.6)	1901	Swing	47	31	26
Rt. 3 Bridge (Rutherford Ave.)[c]	Rutherford (11.8)	1949	Bascule	125	40	35

Douglas O. Mead (Union Ave.) Bridge	Passaic (13.2)	1897	Swing	60	18	13
Aycrigg Avenue Bridge[b]	Passaic (13.5)	d	Draw	62	3	19
Gregory Avenue Bridge	Passaic (14.0)	1906	Swing	71	17	12
Second Street Bridge (Market Street)	Passaic (14.7)	1930	Fixed (Bascule)	100	10	5
W. Eighth Street Bridge	Passaic (15.3)	1914	Fixed (Bascule)	70	10	5
Garfield Highway (Wall Street Bridge)	Passaic (15.9)	1898	Fixed	78	10	5
Monroe Street	Passaic (16.2)	d	Fixed	d	3	12
Sherman Street	Passaic (16.8)		Fixed	d	3	20
Clifton Highway Bridge	Passaic (17.1)	d	Fixed	d	3	12

Notes:
[a] Numbers in parentheses represent the clearance when the bridge is open.
[b] Indicates a bridge that has been removed.
[c] Indicates a bridge that has been reconstructed (date is most recent construction).
[d] Data currently unavailable.

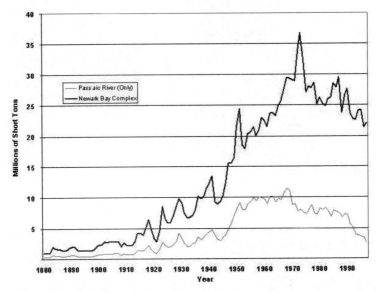

Figure 6-1. Commercial shipping volumes for the Passaic River and Newark Bay, 1880–1997.

The Newark Bay Complex includes Newark Bay, the Passaic River, and the Hackensack River. Prior to 1929, tonnage was reported only for Newark Bay Complex as a whole. For 1880 to 1928, we assume that "Passaic River (only)" tonnage is 33 percent of the volume of the Newark Bay Complex, which is the Passaic River's share from 1929 to 1997.

Sources: USACE, 1900; 1907; 1912; 1913; 1914; 1915; 1916; 1917; 1922; 1953; 1966; 1980; U.S. Coast Guard Bridge Administration, 1984; U.S. Department of Commerce, 1990; USACE, 1997.

reached its peak shipping volume of 36.7 million tons in 1973. Shipping activity has since declined.

Contaminants

Urbanization and industrialization following the Civil War led to widespread contamination of the Passaic River by industrial chemicals and municipal sewage. In 1872, a report to the Board of Public Works of Jersey City described the Passaic River water as "highly offensive to both smell and taste" and having "a shocking degree of contamination" by organic matter (JCWS, 1873; Leeds, 1887). Engineers reported "demonstrable contamination by filth and refuse of every description" (Leeds, 1887). In 1910 the mouth of the River was "black from the sewage and manufacturing wastes" (NOAA, 1981).

Early industries on the lower Passaic River and its tributaries included metals refining, dye manufacturing, tanning, soap and candle production, lumber processing, hat manufacturing, carriage building, and shoe making (Leary, 1891; Pierson, 1917). The industrial revolution of the late 1800s expanded some industries and added others such as petroleum processing, chemical production, and paper and textile milling. Metal works included copper rolling and wire mills, silver manufacturing, and platinum refining (Jacobson, 1958; Cunningham, 1988). An 1894 survey counted 79 mills (of all types) on the River and its tributaries (Brydon, 1974).

The Dundee Dam built in 1858, and high consumption levels of industries and municipalities upstream, dramatically reduced freshwater flow in the River. The low flow concentrated pollution, increasing its impacts. Leakage from oil tanks was frequent. When a pipeline crossing Saddle River burst in the late 1800s, oil covered the surface of the Passaic River for miles (Jacobson, 1958). In the early 1900s, lightweight fuel oils were spread on marshes to control mosquitoes (Headlee, 1945; Wright, 1988). Electronics manufacture began in the early 1900s in Newark. Around 1910, anti-fouling marine paints that contained the toxic metal, mercury, were developed and used on boats and other structures on the River. Copper fungicide applications on farmland in the watershed peaked in the 1940s (Rod *et al.*, 1989) when a considerable agricultural acreage still drained to the River.

In the spring of 1880 a carbolic acid spill from the Kingsland Paper Mill contaminated the River, creating a water scare in Newark (Leeds, 1887). Passaic River historian, Stuart Galishoff (1970), described the event:

> *"Citizens in all sections complained that the water smelled like creosote, tasted 'fishy', and had an odd color. An investigation disclosed that the water was being contaminated by carbolic acid from the Kingsland paper mill located on Third River, some two miles above the Newark intake. The city brought an indictment against the mill for creating a public nuisance and compelled the company to stop discharging its wastes into the river."*

Mill officials argued that effects of the spill were negligible because the River was already heavily contaminated, and that carbolic acid, a disinfectant, would actually make the River *less* dangerous to public health. The court ruled against the mill (Leeds, 1887; Galishoff, 1970).

In addition to industrial contaminants, in the 1880s and 1890s, the volume of raw sewage entering the Passaic increased substantially (Newark News, 1956; Galishoff, 1970; Brydon, 1974). In 1894, one-third of the Passaic River's total flow was untreated sewage (Brydon, 1974). A drought that summer worsened conditions. Acid fumes "blistered the paint of houses along the river and caused an epidemic of nose-bleeding and nausea in Newark" (Galishoff, 1970). Houses adjacent to the River were deserted (Newark News, 1956; Galishoff, 1970). The 1897 report of the Passaic Valley Sewerage Commission described the pollution of the Passaic River:

"... *From ... [the Great Falls] to Newark Bay, its pollution is enormous, constant, and increasing yearly. Seventy million gallons of sewage befoul it daily.*"

Table 6-3 lists the major sewage-generating cities at the time of the 1897 report. All sewage from Paterson and Passaic and some from Newark and Kearny was piped to the Passaic.

Throughout the 1870s and 1880s municipal governments worked to identify and remedy pollution on the Passaic (ISC, 1939; Suszkowski, 1978). In February 1880, Newark passed a law prohibiting individuals and manufacturers from polluting waterways used for drinking water (Galishoff, 1970; Brydon, 1974). But pollution, both point and non-point, continued to impact the River.

In October 1881, Newark organized the Board of Inspection of the Pollution of the Passaic River and its Tributaries, known as the Pollution Board, to address public health threats from pollution. On December 31, 1881, the Chief Engineer of Jersey City predicted that the Pollution Board would return the River to its original state and both Jersey City and Newark would have

Table 6-3.   Major sewage-generating cities in 1897

City	Sewage[a]
Paterson	26.0
Passaic	8.5
Newark	34.0
Kearny (Arlington)	7.0

Notes:
[a] In millions of gallons per day.
Source: Passaic Valley Sewerage Commission, 1897.

"a pure and abundant water supply" within a few years (Galishoff, 1970). Initially, the Pollution Board made progress, but early successes were overwhelmed as pollution increased.

Municipalities and industries actively hindered the Pollution Board's efforts to cleanse the River. The Pollution Board tried to persuade the cities of Passaic and Belleville to use sanitary sewage disposal, but they continued discharging into nearby tributaries. Other cities, including Paterson and Newark, used the Passaic River directly to discharge sewage. The Pollution Board legislation was ineffective in preventing factory owners from polluting the River. Legal notices were ignored, and civil actions proceeded slowly. Factory owners protected each other when the Pollution Board threatened criminal actions (Galishoff, 1970).

Responding to a community petition, Professor Albert Leeds of the Stevens Institute of Technology in Hoboken studied Passaic River pollution in 1887. At the time, Jersey City residents were already convinced that the water was unfit for consumption. Thousands of people refused to drink Passaic River water at all, and thousands of others filtered and boiled the water before they used it (Leeds, 1887; Jacobson, 1958; Galishoff, 1970). In response to contamination of the Passaic, many Newark residents dug their own wells, but by 1890 over 1,000 of the more than 1,500 wells were contaminated (Galishoff, 1988). Professor Leeds identified sewage, oil, and industrial discharges such as dyes, acids, and chemicals as major pollutants in the Passaic River (Leeds, 1887). When asked to list, in order, the major sources of pollution to the Passaic River, Professor Leeds said, "the city of Passaic, the city of Paterson, the oil pipeline at Saddle River, Third River, the town of Belleville, Second River, and the city of Newark" (Leeds, 1887). As part of his investigation,

Professor Leeds developed a map depicting the sources of pollution to the Passaic River as of the mid-1880s (Figure 6-2).

Despite early attempts to remedy the River's contamination, by 1897, Passaic River "fisheries had been destroyed," and "the River had ceased to be desirable for pleasure purposes, boating, bathing, etc." (Passaic Valley Sewerage Commission, 1897). Newark abandoned the River as a public water supply (Galishoff, 1970; Brydon, 1974). With public pressure relaxed, industrial pollution increased (Cunningham, 1988). President Woodrow Wilson, in a 1910 campaign speech said that one could get "a sniff of the history of the Passaic River from the roadside, as it is lifted to heaven out of the very waters of the stream" (Noble, 1959). "Disgusted by the sight and smell of raw sewage, residents turned their backs and even their park benches away from the river" (Peet and Johnson, 1996).

In response, the Passaic Valley trunk sewer line was completed in 1924. The trunk intercepted sewage from towns along the River and carried it directly to New York Harbor. Passaic Valley residents expected that the trunk sewer would improve water quality and revive recreation (Star-Ledger, 1929; Star-Ledger, 1946; Brydon, 1974). All municipalities from Paterson to the mouth of the River were included in the trunk sewer plan. Untreated waste that had contaminated the Passaic River now bypassed it.

After the trunk sewer line was built, the Great Depression slowed industrial and urban growth, and population levels stabilized temporarily. Water quality improved and recreation briefly revived (Brydon, 1974).

Water quality declined again during the massive industrial buildup for World War II and the postwar economic expansion.

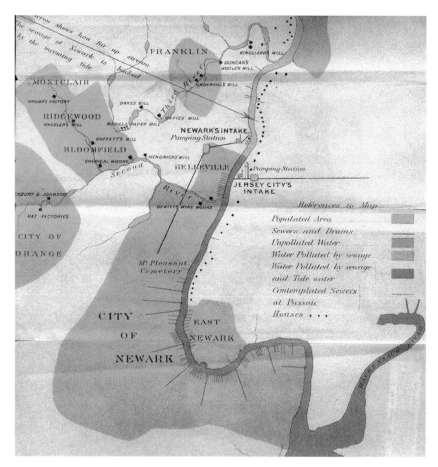

Figure 6-2. Map depicting known sources of pollution to the lower Passaic River—mid 1880s (Leeds, 1887).

A report by the Center for Analysis of Public Issues in 1972 (Beale, 1972), titled *Pollution Control on the Passaic River*, concluded that the Passaic River basin supported a wealth of "pollution industries—chemicals, paper products, refining, and electroplating (cyanide)" (Beale, 1972) (Table 6-4).

By the late 1960s the trunk sewer was overwhelmed by population growth and sewage was again a major problem on the Passaic. In 1967, 40 million gallons of effluent per day were discharged from treatment plants above Little Falls, accounting for 5.6% of the average river flow that year. On September 29, 1967, when river flow was particularly low, effluent accounted for 41% (Princeton University Students, 1971). In 1974 and 1975, combined storm water and sewage overflows into the Passaic River exceeded 7 billion gallons for the year. Another 2 billion gallons

Table 6-4.   Industries in municipalities bordering the Passaic River below Paterson, New Jersey, in 1970

Municipality	Paper Mills	Petroleum Plants	Dye, Paint, Chemicals	Electroplating
Belleville	2	0	10	1
Bloomfield	4	0	2	1
Clifton	13	2	26	1
East Newark	0	0	4	0
East Rutherford	2	0	17	1
East Paterson	4	0	9	0
East Orange	1	0	3	0
Fair Lawn	0	0	10	1
Garfield	5	0	1	2
Harrison	4	0	3	0
Hawthorne	0	0	7	2
Kearny	2	1	16	1
Lyndhurst	1	0	4	2
Newark	24	8	103	28
Passaic	1	0	11	2
Paterson	4	1	80	5
Rutherford	0	0	6	0
Wallington	0	0	2	2
Total	**67**	**12**	**314**	**49**

Source: Beale, 1972

of storm water and sanitary overflow went into Newark Bay, and 40 billion gallons of storm flow "also with a measurable pollutional load on the river" (Elson T. Killam Associates, Inc., 1976) were released.

Industrial pollution, combined with increasing sewage discharges, led the New Jersey Environmental Protection Commissioner to conclude in 1970, that "in many respects, the water of the lower Passaic is deadly" (Beale, 1972). Murray Stein, Assistant Commissioner of the Federal Water Pollution Control Administration, examined the River in 1969 and concluded, "It is a dead river and ranks with rivers like the Cuyahoga, the Buffalo, and the Houston Ship Canal, and it is a disgrace to the United States." Several months later, Stein remarked that, "This is a fetid, polluted stream that offends human sensibilities and is a danger to health and welfare" (Beale, 1972). In 1970, the USEPA declared the Passaic River the "second most polluted river in America," behind only the Cuyahoga, which had caught fire in 1969 (Peet and Johnson, 1996).

In 1980, one of the Passaic Valley Sewerage Commission trunk lines ruptured and the state allowed the agency to dump half a billion gallons of raw sewage into the Passaic (Walz, 1993). Daniel Van Abs of the NJDEP stated in 1987 that:

"The river's major pollutant is poorly treated household sewage filtering in from overtaxed sewer systems upstream from the area being rehabilitated [referring to a Passaic River Restoration Project on the lower Passaic]. Waste from the river's 3,000 industries hasn't been a serious problem since a sewer trunk line was installed more than 50 years ago to collect most of those discharges." (The Record, 1987).

Water contamination remains a concern along the Passaic River. Historically, the region was plagued by poor water quality—low dissolved oxygen (DO), high biochemical oxygen demand (BOD), high nutrient levels, ammonia concentrations, and fecal coliform levels (USACE, 1987). NOAA (1981) reported water quality steadily deteriorated throughout the first half of the 20th century. By the mid-1970s, DO concentrations were low throughout the NY/NJ Harbor Estuary (Keller *et al.*, 1991). In the Passaic River, DO was as low as 0.1 mg/L and by 1977 water quality was so poor that the state closed the lower portion of the River to swimming and fishing (NOAA, 1981; NJMSC, 1987).

Several of the region's most historically polluted sewer outfalls are located along the lower Passaic River (HydroQual, 1995; Killam, 1983; Shear *et al.*, 1996; Huntley *et al.*, 1997; Iannuzzi *et al.*, 1997; Walker *et al.*, 1999). In 1912, the Metropolitan Sewage Commission estimated that Newark Bay received 13 million gallons per day (MGD) of wastewater. By the mid-1970s, NOAA (1978) estimated the Bay was receiving inputs of 58.5 MGD of wastewater (Suszkowski, 1978). In the 1970s, Newark Bay and the Hackensack and Passaic Rivers received domestic and industrial wastewater discharges that accounted for 13% of the total input into the Bay (NOAA, 1978). An estimated $1.3 billion has been spent over the past 25 years maintaining antiquated wastewater treatment plants along the Passaic River. The Passaic Valley Sewerage Commission used more than 14,000 pounds of chlorine a day in 1984 to treat microbes in water from the Passaic River (Peet and Johnson, 1996).

In 1971, the state classified the tidal portion of the Passaic River, below Dundee Dam, as TW-3—"Used primarily for nav-

91

igation, not recreation . . . suitable for fish survival and the passage of anadromous fish" (Beale, 1972). Under TW-3 classification, toxic substances should not be present at concentrations that cause fish mortality, and DO levels should not drop below 3.0 ppm. These standards were not met on the Passaic River. DO levels frequently fell far below the standard. "A complete depletion of oxygen was recorded near Harrison in both 1968 and 1969, with levels below 2.0 characterizing the remainder of the tidal waters down to Newark Bay." ". . . It should be clear . . . that these water quality standards are not being met in much of the Passaic Basin . . . During the summer recreation months, these waters are certainly not fit for primary contact and are occasionally unfit for fish life" (Beale, 1972).

Since 1975, federal and state pollution controls and the efforts of local community-action groups have improved conditions on the Passaic River (NJDEP, 1987). The regional population has stabilized, sewage treatment facilities have upgraded their capacities, industry has reduced point-source emissions, and manufacturing activity has declined (Crawford *et al.*, 1994). The effect is an improved Passaic River, one that is more hospitable to some forms of recreation and aquatic life (Passaic River Coalition, 1983). Members of the Passaic River Restoration Project (PRRP), a community group organized by the Passaic River Coalition toured the River in 1983:

> "*Officials on the trip were impressed with the open space along the river, its beauty, and potential. Many participants commented on how much cleaner the Passaic River is today than previously. One old timer said that in the evenings the river is frequently alive with jumping fish when ten years ago [1973] there were none and water lilies have returned to the banks.*"

The community initiated many clean-up efforts, as this 1996 *Star-Ledger* (Peet and Johnson, 1996) article suggests:

". . . Then came the 1980s, New Jersey's age of environmentalism. More than $4 billion and thousands of volunteer man-hours have been spent cleaning up the Passaic. Slowly, the river is recovering and its rebirth reinforces the possibility that the state can shed its own toxic baggage."

However, the same Passaic River tour that yielded the observations described previously also yielded the following comments:

"Abandoned barges, old tires, shopping carts, cars and trash were also visible as well as rotting bulkheads. Fishermen and boaters complained that someone is throwing tires on rims into the river intentionally . . ." (Passaic River Coalition, 1983)

A number of studies have been conducted to characterize the chemical contamination of the Passaic River and Newark Bay, including the ongoing Superfund investigation being conducted by USEPA (Meyerson *et al.*, 1981; McCormick *et al.*, 1983; Ayres and Rod, 1986; NJDEP, 1987; Finley *et al.*, 1990; Bopp and Simpson, 1991; Bonnevie *et al.*, 1992; Bonnevie *et al.*, 1993; Gunster *et al.*, 1993; Huntley *et al.*, 1993; Wenning *et al.*, 1993a,b,c; Bonnevie *et al.*, 1994; Crawford *et al.*, 1995; Gillis *et al.*, 1995; Huntley *et al.*, 1995; Iannuzzi and Wenning, 1995; Iannuzzi *et al.*, 1995; USEPA, 1999). In addition, NJDEP (1980; 1983; 1985a; 1990; 1993) and Iannuzzi *et al.*, (1996) investigated contamination of fish and shellfish from the Passaic River. Hundreds of chemicals were released into the Passaic River during the latter half of the 19th century and throughout the 20th century. These include heavy metals such as cadmium, copper, lead, mercury, and zinc; poly-cyclic aromatic hydrocarbons (PAHs); pesticides such as chlor-dane and dichlorodiphenyltrichloroethane (DDT); polychlori-nated biphenyls (PCBs); polychlorinated dibenzo-*p*-dioxins and dibenzofurans (PCDD/Fs); and volatile and semi-volatile com-pounds. A number of these chemicals have exceeded available sediment quality benchmarks at some time during the last century (Figure 6-3). These benchmarks are concentrations of each chem-ical above which adverse biological effects are expected at some level. A large number of chemicals are present in the River for which such effects-based benchmarks do not exist. Many con-taminants still reside in the sediments and aquatic organisms of the River, and many are still being discharged.

Historical metals concentrations in sediments of the lower part of the River have ranged on average from 0.2 to 27.5 parts per million (ppm) for cadmium, 13 to 1,220 ppm for chromium, 24 to 913 ppm for copper, 3 to 852 ppm for lead, 0.1 to 13.2 ppm for mercury, 10 to 124 ppm for nickel, and 30 to 1,910 ppm for zinc. Metals generally increased in the River during the indus-trial expansions before and after World War II and decreased to-ward the end of the last century.

Historical concentrations of total DDT ranged from 0.006 to over 300 ppm. Concentrations of high-molecular-weight PAHs ranged from non-detect to over 105 ppm, and concentrations of low-molecular-weight PAHs ranged from non-detect to nearly 130 ppm.

Historical sources of metals to the Passaic River include smelters (copper, lead, nickel), and paint manufacturers and dye manufacturers (cadmium, copper, lead, mercury, zinc), electro-plating industries (cadmium, zinc), and petroleum refineries

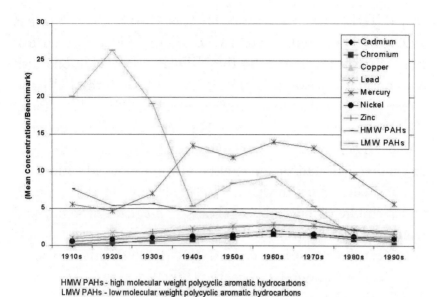

HMW PAHs - high molecular weight polycyclic aromatic hydrocarbons
LMW PAHs - low molecular weight polycyclic aromatic hydrocarbons

Figure 6-3. Ratios of sediment concentrations to sediment quality benchmarks for select pollutants

(lead) (Wenning *et al.* 1994). PAHs in the environment can come from natural sources such as wildfires, and man-made sources such as fossil fuel combustion, petroleum refineries, and creosote wood preserving facilities. Although PCBs were not manufactured in the Passaic area, these compounds were used extensively in products such as adhesives, insulating materials, flame retardants, lubricants, paints, pigments, and oil varnishes (Wenning *et al.* 1994). DDT and other pesticides and herbicides were manufactured by industries along the River during and after World War II. PCDD/Fs are by-products of pesticide and other industrial manufacturing processes.

PCBs were identified in fish from the lower Passaic River in 1977, and in 1982 the NJDEP issued a fish-consumption advisory (NJDEP, 1980; 1985b; NJDEP/NJDHSS, 1997; NJDEP, 1999). In 1983, dioxin (i.e., PCDD/Fs) was identified in fish from the River and in 1984 the NJDEP issued additional fish consumption advisories (NJDEP, 1985a,b). Both the PCB and dioxin fish consumption advisories remain in place today (NJDEP, 1999; USEPA, 1999). For the Passaic River between Dundee Dam and Newark Bay the advisories warn both high-risk individuals and the general population to avoid eating any fish or shellfish from the River. High-risk individuals include infants, children under the age of 15, pregnant women, and women of childbearing age. In addition, advisories warn people not to eat or harvest blue crabs (NJDEP, 1999), although some urban anglers ignore the advisories (Pflugh, 1996).

Clearly, releases of chemical contaminants have adversely affected the Passaic River and reduced its ecological and human use services. The institution of fishing and shellfishing advisories by the NJDEP over the last 25 years is evidence that chemical contaminants have directly harmed the River, and that these releases need to be addressed before the River can recover. In additon, sewage contamination has caused serious problems in the past and continues to be an issue today. Combined sewer overflows (outfalls) and stormwater run-off remain key sources of chemical contamination to the Passaic River, in addition to the myriad sources previously discussed. In order to continue the progress made in recent years in managing and restoring the River, the cumulative impacts of human activities on water quality need to be addressed.

7

FISH AND SHELLFISH
The Victims of Industrialization and Urbanization

"Our struggle is for the future: ours and that of the fish."

J. Kurien (1998)

THE PASSAIC RIVER ONCE HAD an abundant fishery, including a wide variety of species. In his 1885 history of Belleville, Holmes called the Passaic River "the great natural aquarium." Shad, white and yellow perch, suckers, catfish, bass of several species, salmon, pickerel, herring, various sunfishes, sturgeon, eels, smelt, "roach," and chubs were caught in the clear waters of the River in the early 1800s (Forester, 1854; Brown, 1857; Holmes, 1885; Holmes, 1890; Rankin, 1930; Esselborn, 1958; Brydon, 1974). It has been estimated that about 200 species of edible fish and shellfish existed in the Newark region prior to

European settlement (McCormick and Quinn, 1975; Santoro *et al.*, 1980; Quinn, 1998)

Early residents of the area relied on fish and shellfish for food (Quinn, 1997). Anglers could catch a "basket-full" in one hour with a rod and line, and fish would come to the surface and feed when fishermen rinsed bait from their hands (Holmes, 1885; 1890). Fishermen from around the region traveled to Newark Bay to enter fishing contests (Lee, 1902). Green Island once marked the spot of a famous striped bass fishing reef in the Passaic River (Rankin, 1930).

The Passaic River also supported a well established commercial fishery for smelt and shad (Rankin, 1930). Smelts were caught "by the wagonload" and "over 700" shad could be caught in a single sweep of a seine (Holmes, 1885; 1890). Passaic River shad fetched high prices in nearby towns and cities (Earll, 1887). Atlantic sturgeon were caught in the River and sold as "Albany beef" (Holmes, 1885; 1890).

Fish Resources

Declining fish populations began to be reported in the 1880s. By all accounts, declines were rapid and severe. The last report of abundant fish in the lower part of the Passaic River was written in 1873 in a Report to the Joint Commission on the Water Supply of the Cities of Newark and Jersey City (JCWS, 1873). While it did not mention specific species, the report stated that the lower portion of the Passaic River near the sewer outfall "swarm[ed]" with fish which fed on the organic matter.

In his 1885 book entitled *A Brief History of Belleville*, Holmes described how abundant and varied fish populations had been, writing in the past tense, but he did not note when the decline began. In 1887, shad caught in Newark Bay had lost their value because of an oil taint in the flesh (Earll, 1887), and "fisherman complained loudly against the emptying of [coal oil] into the rivers." (Earll, 1887). By 1892, much fish life had disappeared from the River, and in 1897 only a few hardy species lived in the Passaic (Passaic Valley Sewerage Commission, 1897). Shad and smelt were among the fish that abandoned the River. For a few years before 1887, the shad catch was very light and the smelt catch was quite insignificant (Earll, 1887). By the time the 1905 Report of the Commissioner of the Fisheries was written, the Passaic River and Newark Bay were no longer listed as commercial fish sources. A 1926 survey of the area by the U.S. War Department declared the "fish life destroyed" (Hurley, 1992).

The precipitous decline of fish in the Passaic can be traced to several sources:

- Destruction of wetland habitats that provided foraging, spawning, nursery areas, and refuges;
- Decreased vegetated habitat, increased turbidity, and loss of benthic invertebrates for food caused by repeated dredging of sediments from the River;
- Chronic pollution of the waters by sewage and other wastes;
- Chronically low DO levels;
- Toxic levels of several chemical contaminants.

The BOD created by the sewage was one of the main causes of the chronically low levels of DO found in the River (Crawford *et al.*, 1994). Other sources of BOD were paper mill effluents and releases from oil refineries, pipelines, and storage facilities. Paper-mill effluent contains organic materials that are composed of wood sugars, fatty acids, lignin, and cellulose. Oil and refinery effluents contain other energy-rich organic matter. These highly concentrated organic molecules make an excellent food for microbes. Microbial metabolism accounts for the "enormous" BOD of paper-mill effluents and oil spills (Burger, 1994).

Oxygen dissolved in water is a critically important requirement for aquatic life and is measured in units of milligrams (mg) of oxygen per liter (L) of water. DO concentrations below 5 mg/L are lethal to most fish species and higher concentrations (up to 12 or 13 mg/L, where water is "saturated" and unable to absorb more oxygen) are better. Low (but not lethal) DO levels can inhibit growth. DO concentrations in the Passaic River measured in 1909 averaged 0.33 mg/L. Throughout the early 1900s, DO concentrations in Newark Bay were less than 3 mg/L. Because fish can avoid waters with low DO concentrations, portions of the River with chronically low DO were "lost" habitat for many fish and invertebrate species (Paling, 1971; Cerrato, 1986; McHugh *et al.*, 1990; Diaz and Rosenberg, 1995). Ammonia, which was also present in the Passaic River at high levels (Jacobson, 1958), is toxic to fish, can inhibit their growth, and is actively avoided.

While industrial effluent and sewage discharges into the River made the River incompatible with aquatic life, the loss of tributaries and their associated wetlands also had dramatic effects on fish. Tidal marsh wetlands are very productive ecosystems and "may contribute more to total ecosystem production than suggested by the absolute area they occupy within estuaries" (Shenker and Dean, 1979; Kneib, 1997). Tidal creeks and marshes provide vital habitat for resident fish that live in the

River year around, like mummichogs, and migratory fish that return to the River seasonally, like American eel, striped bass, and Atlantic silversides. Fish used the tidal creek wetlands for foraging, spawning, nurseries, and refuge (Kneib, 1997). Tidal creeks support more diverse fish communities than either streams or rivers (Able *et al.*, 1996).

It is likely that wetland and tributary losses brought about the severe declines and losses of fish in the latter half of the 19th century and first half of the 20th century. In the mid-1800s, Wheeler's, Maple Island, and Pierson Creeks were cut off from the Bay by tide gates (Figure 7-1). This eliminated tidal flow to and from the marshes, lowered salinity, and kept estuarine fish out of the creeks. Energy no longer flowed from these creeks to the Bay (Talbot *et al.*, 1986). Some marsh-estuarine fish species, including mummichogs and other killifish (*Fundulus* spp.), must utilize the marsh surface to obtain a portion of their energy requirement (Weisberg and Lotrich, 1982). Excluding tidal flow (and thus fish) from the marshes would have dramatically reduced their populations.

As discussed in Chapter 5, marshes were ditched for mosquito control throughout the 1800s and early 1900s. Ditching eliminated smaller tributaries, which are important habitat for fish. Unditched marshes contain more valuable habitat and are inundated by tidewater longer than ditched marshes. Complex edge habitat in unditched creeks is used extensively by almost all fish species (Kneib, 1993; 1997). When the tributaries were completely destroyed by either filling or conversion into sewer systems, they and their associated marsh habitats were lost for fish production. That fish populations remain limited in diversity and abundance, despite water quality improvements over the

Figure 7-1. Example of tide gate on a salt marsh in New Jersey (Headlee, 1945; with permission from Rutgers University Press).

past two decades, demonstrates the importance of the now nearly non-existent wetland and tributary habitat for fish production.

In addition to marsh habitat, the vitality of the Passaic River's sediment is key to the survival of fish. Dredging impacted fish by destroying communities of bottom-dwelling invertebrates (a favored food for fish), removing SAV (an important habitat component), and remobilizing contaminants that had been buried in the sediments. Portions of Newark Bay were dredged in all but 4 of the 30 years between 1910 and 1940 (Suszkowski, 1978) and thus had little chance to recover.

Dredging and degraded water quality caused near total losses of SAV in the Passaic River by direct physical removal and reduction of underwater light levels, which inhibits SAV growth (Kennish, 1992). SAV is important for fish habitat because it provides food and serves as refuge for smaller species and juveniles (Rozas and Odum, 1987). The Passaic River was once full of SAV between Newark and Belleville (Jacobson, 1958).

Surface and buried sediments (representing deposits from many years time) from the Passaic River contain a number of chemical contaminants that have degraded the sediment quality of the River. These toxic chemicals negatively impact the communities of bottom-dwelling invertebrates. These invertebrates are an important food source for fish, and impacts to the invertebrates would have been reflected in impacts to the fish.

The toll of all of these ills became evident toward the end of the 20th century. Only four fish species appeared to exist in the lower Passaic River in the 1970s (NJBFF, 1981). In the mid-1980s, the Passaic was so polluted that even the carp and catfish populations, "the kings of pollutant-resistant fish" appeared to be depressed (Peet and Johnson, 1996). Fish were "literally gasping for breath in a river choked nearly empty of oxygen from sewage and chemicals dumped by upstream wastewater plants" (Peet and Johnson, 1996). Today, at least 27 species of fish live in the Passaic (Peet and Johnson, 1996). But this improved fish community falls far short of the abundance and diversity that existed before industrialization and development.

Shellfish Resources

Shellfish historically present in the lower Passaic River and Newark Bay included oysters, shrimp of several kinds, clams, and crabs. In the early 1800s, Newark Bay was "oyster-rich"

(Smith, 1887; McCay, 1998). Thousands of bushels of seed oysters were harvested from Newark Bay and planted elsewhere, including San Francisco Bay, Great South Bay, and New York Bay (Ingersoll, 1887). In 1882, over 175,000 bushels of oyster seed was harvested over a period of seven months (MacKenzie, 1992). In contrast, crabs harvested from the Bay were generally taken for local consumption (Earll, 1887). Crustaceans and fish were a substantial part of the diet of local residents until the late 1800s (Smith, 1887; Quinn, 1997). Shrimp were plentiful in the Passaic River in the early 1800s (Esselborn, 1958).

The oyster harvest was hit hard by over-fishing and pollution. New Jersey authorities blamed declining oyster production in Newark Bay on the tongers, who collected seed oysters for transplant using long handled clamps called "oyster tongs." The tongers did not always return the shells to the bottoms to provide attachment sites for the next generation of oyster larvae (Esselborn, 1958). Year-round harvesting contributed to the decline, and in 1870 the New Jersey legislature passed the Act for the Preservation of Clams and Oysters, which made it illegal to take clams and oysters between May 1 and September 1 (Brydon, 1968). Nonetheless, in 1882, the seed harvest had fallen by 100,000 bushels from the previous year. In 1921, oystering was stopped completely to protect human health because of Newark Bay's pollution (McCay, 1998).

Shellfish in the lower Passaic River and Newark Bay struggled throughout the 19th and 20th centuries because of chronic sewage pollution and low DO levels; toxic levels of chemical contaminants; habitat destruction from shoreline modification and wetlands loss; and sediment smothering from dredging activities (Steimle and Caracciolo-Ward, 1989). Some species were impacted by the increasing salinity gradient that was caused by reduced freshwater flow.

As discussed previously, sewage pollution and other factors resulted in chronically low DO concentrations in the Passaic River and Newark Bay. Several crustacean species, including blue crabs and penaeid shrimp are extremely sensitive to low DO levels (Stickle *et al.*, 1989). Areas of the River with hypoxic (low oxygen) conditions were "out of bounds" for many species, contributing to population declines.

Dredging of the River and Bay impacted shellfish by physically damaging the bottom and by mobilizing smothering sediments. Benthic communities of dredged areas can require six months to a year to fully recover, and some communities take up to three years to recover. Furthermore, dredging would have remobilized contaminants that had been buried in the sediments, and increased ammonia concentrations in water.

Some shellfish, such as shrimp, need access to marshes or SAV for part of their life cycle. Brown shrimp, for example, selectively inhabit salt marsh cord grass (*Spartina alterniflora*) during most of the year (Minello and Zimmerman, 1991). Tidal gates cut off wetland nurseries for migratory shrimp species. Edge habitat was destroyed by ditching and filling tidal creeks, impacting migratory species that fed or sheltered in the marshes. Wetland and tributary losses were substantial (Tables 5-2 and 5-3). Habitat constraints continue to limit shellfish populations today in these waterways despite improvements in water quality.

Today, the blue crab, a relatively pollution-tolerant crustacean, is the primary shellfish species inhabiting the Passaic River and, along with the mummichog, represents a substantial portion of the biomass in the River. Repopulating the Passaic

River with the large variety and quantity of fish and shellfish found in its distant past is a lofty goal. Attaining that goal will require an integrated effort that addresses the wide range of problems affecting fish and shellfish. Clearly, the recovery of some fish species in the River can be tied to improvements made in water quality, including increasing DO and making the River inhabitable for many fish. However, additional factors such as wetland destruction, tributary degradation, and pollution also affect fish viability and need to be addressed if the River's fishery is to be restored.

8

WILDLIFE
What has Survived the
Urban Transition?

"Humans have proven to be versatile exterminators
in recent centuries . . ."

C.L. Redman (1999)

THE WETLANDS, FORESTS, AND FIELDS of northern New Jersey once provided expansive habitat for birds, reptiles, and mammals. Resident species used the area for breeding, foraging, and cover. Birds, in particular, were well studied by ornithology experts and birding clubs in New Jersey and New York. Numerous texts and journals document the formerly abundant bird life of the area (Lawrence, 1867; Shriner, 1896; New Jersey State Museum, 1903; Chapman, 1906; Abbott, 1907; Bent, 1919; Urner, 1921; Urner, 1923; Urner, 1925; Bent, 1927; Bent, 1929; Griscom, 1929; Urner 1935; Bent, 1938; McKeever, 1941; Cruickshank, 1942; McKeever, 1946; Fables, 1955; Siebenheller, 1981; Siebenheller and Siebenheller, 1983; Barrett, 1990a).

Birds

Historically, the Newark area marshes and meadows were home to a wide variety of birds. The species found there included raptors such as the northern harrier (marsh hawk) and short-eared owls; wading birds such as great blue and green herons and American bittern; shore birds such as killdeer; marsh birds such as rails, coots, and red-wing blackbird; and meadow birds like the meadowlark and sparrows. Many birds used the habitats around the lower Passaic River and Newark Bay during seasonal migrations. Tables 8-1 and 8-2 summarize bird use of habitats in the Newark Bay region. As with fish, however, overharvest, landscape alterations, and habitat impacts combined to diminish bird life in the area.

Bird populations plummeted when hunters conducted mass killings for the food market and the millinery trade in the late 1800s and early 1900s (Dutcher, 1886). Egret plumage was particularly sought after for hats. Entire bodies of smaller birds or wings and feathers of larger species were designed into fancy hats of the day. Great blue herons were hunted intensively for their long feather plumage (Peet and Johnson, 1996). Other species nearly extirpated in the region by over-hunting include the common tern, Forster's tern, piping plover, ruddy turnstone, red knot, pectoral sandpiper, dunlin, eastern dowitcher, laughing gull, least tern, and Caspian tern (Cruickshank, 1942; Barrett, 1990b).

Protective legislation was passed in 1903, at the urging of the Audubon Society and other conservation organizations. The law

Table 8-1. Historical breeding birds and key habitats in the Newark Bay region

Species	Urban/ Suburban	Open Meadow	Riparian Forest	Emergent Wetland	Shoreline/ Nearshore	Lakes/ Ponds
Bittern, American						✓
Bittern, Least				✓		
Blackbird, Red-Winged		✓	✓	✓		
Bobolink		✓				
Coot, American				✓	✓	✓
Crow, Fish			✓	✓	✓	
Flycatcher, Acadian			✓			
Gnatcatcher, Blue-Gray		✓				
Grebe, Pied-Billed				✓		✓
Grosbeak, Blue		✓	✓			
Harrier, Northern		✓		✓		
Heron, Great Blue				✓		✓
Heron, Green				✓		✓
Heron, Little Blue				✓		✓
Heron, Tricolored				✓	✓	✓
Killdeer	✓	✓		✓	✓	
Kingfisher, Eastern Belted				✓		✓

Table 8-1. (continued)

Species	Urban/ Suburban	Open Meadow	Riparian Forest	Emergent Wetland	Shoreline/ Nearshore	Lakes/ Ponds
Lark, Northern Horned	✓					
Meadowlark, Eastern		✓				
Moorhen, Common		✓		✓		✓
Owl, Short-Ear				✓		
Rail, Clapper				✓		
Rail, King				✓		
Rail, Virginia				✓		
Sandpiper, Spotted		✓				✓
Sora				✓		
Sparrow, Grasshopper		✓				
Sparrow, Savannah		✓		✓		
Sparrow, Sharp-Tailed				✓		
Sparrow, Swamp				✓		
Whip-poor-will, Eastern			✓			
Willet				✓		
Wren, Marsh				✓		
Yellowthroat, Common		✓		✓		

Sources: Leck, 1984; Allen *et al.*, 1987; Ehrlich *et al.*, 1988.

Table 8-2. Historical migratory birds and key habitats in the Newark Bay region

Species	Urban/ Suburban Meadows	Open Meadows	Riparian Forest	Emergent Wetland	Shoreline/ Nearshore	Lakes/ Ponds
Avocet, American				✓		✓
Bunting, Snow					✓	
Canvasback				✓	✓	✓
Dowitcher, Short-Billed				✓	✓	
Dunlin					✓	
Godwit, Hudsonian					✓	
Godwit, Marbled				✓		
Goose, Snow				✓		
Gull, Glaucous	✓				✓	
Gull, Herring					✓	
Gull, Iceland					✓	
Gull, Laughing				✓		
Gull, Ring-Billed		✓			✓	✓
Hawk, Rough-Legged	✓	✓			✓	
Knot, Red					✓	
Loon, Red-Throated					✓	✓
Merganser, Red-Breasted					✓	✓
Owl, Snowy	✓				✓	
Phalarope, Red-Necked					✓	✓
Phalarope, Wilson's				✓	✓	✓

Table 8-2. (continued)

Species	Urban/Suburban Meadows	Open Meadows	Riparian Forest	Emergent Wetland	Shoreline/Nearshore	Lakes/Ponds
Plover, Black–Bellied				✓	✓	
Plover, Lesser Golden				✓	✓	
Plover, Semipalmated					✓	✓
Sanderling				✓	✓	
Sandpiper, Pectoral				✓	✓	
Sandpiper, Semipalmated				✓		
Sandpiper, Western				✓	✓	
Shoveler, Northern				✓		
Skimmer, Black				✓		
Snipe, Common				✓		
Tern, Common						✓
Tern, Forster's					✓	
Turnstone, Ruddy					✓	✓
Warbler, Connecticut			✓			
Yellowlegs, Greater		✓		✓	✓	
Yellowlegs, Lesser		✓		✓	✓	

Sources: Leck, 1984; Allen *et al.*, 1987; Ehrlich *et al.*, 1988.

112

offered some protection but was ultimately inadequate. Stricter legislation was passed in 1911 with the Plumage Proviso to existing game laws, "advocated by conservationists as the ultimate in non-game bird protection." In this provision, "no person shall, in New Jersey, kill or catch or have in possession, living or dead, any wild bird other than a game bird, or purchase, offer or expose for sale any such wild bird after it has been caught or killed, and no part of plumage, skin or body of any such bird protected by this section shall be sold or held in possession for sale" (Brydon, 1968). Under this provision, plumage was defined as "any part of feathers, wings, or tail of any bird, including out of State or within State." In 1931, the Weeks-McLean Migratory Bird Bill extended protection to "useful" non-game migratory birds (Brydon, 1968). While these laws prevented extinction, many species did not recover their numbers (Cruickshank, 1942; Brydon, 1968).

Habitat destruction also plagued birds in the region. Noted ornithologist Charles A. Urner presented a paper to the New Jersey Mosquito Extermination Association in 1935 that discussed the effects of mosquito control efforts in the Newark salt marshes on birds (Urner, 1935). Urner observed that ditching and draining marshes destroyed valuable waterfowl and wading bird habitat. He reported that the pied-billed grebe, least bittern, clapper rail, Virginia rail, Florida gallinule, and American coot were lost to the Newark area. American bitterns were still present but in much reduced numbers. Urner predicted that species such as great blue herons, green herons, least sandpipers, greater yellowlegs, Hudsonian curlews, willet, seaside sparrow, and sharp-trailed sparrow would be impacted by ditching and draining.

A.D. Cruickshank confirmed Urner's predicted population

declines seven years later in the 1942 text, *Birds Around New York City: Where and When to Find Them.* Clapper rails, gallinules, American coots, short-eared owls, marsh wrens, red-wing black-birds, sharp-tailed sparrows, northern seaside sparrows, and swamp sparrows were all at dangerously low population levels. Interestingly, bobolink populations briefly increased after the salt marshes were drained, but decreased after common reed invaded the drained areas (Cruickshank, 1942). In 1927, the bobolink was removed from the game bird list, giving the species protection under New Jersey's Plumage Proviso (Brydon, 1968).

In 1955, David Fables, Jr. published the *Annotated List of New Jersey Birds*. He noted that the formerly abundant marbled and Hudsonian godwits were no longer found in Newark area marshes. Other species, including the American bittern, clapper and Virginia rails, short-eared owl, marsh wren, grasshopper sparrow, and seaside sparrow, were declining because wetland habitat in the Passaic River and Newark Bay region was being rapidly depleted. Virginia rails were a summer resident that inhabited the areas at the edge of the salt marshes. Marsh wrens were well distributed in the cat-tail marshes in the meadows but declined as large areas of its habitat were destroyed. Fables noted that the seaside sparrow populations were decreasing because of mosquito extermination work in the marshes along the coast of New Jersey. By the 1920s, migratory bird populations were also impacted by massive and widely distributed oil slicks, and pollution was affecting their food supplies (Hurley, 1992). In addition, garbage disposal in the marshes contributed to avian botulism, another factor that likely contributed to the decline of wading birds (Brydon, 1968).

Wetland and tributary loss impacts on wetland-dependent bird populations are quantified in Table 8-3. The estimates of historical breeding (i.e., adult) bird abundance are derived from wetland area based on information reported by Custer and Osborn (1977). While the precise relationship differs for various species and waterways, it is certain that birds that historically inhabited the Passaic River and Newark Bay depended on the wetlands and tributaries for breeding and foraging. This analysis suggests that there were severe declines and losses of bird populations that occurred in these waterways throughout the latter half of the 19th century and first half of the 20th century (Table 8-3). Table 8-4 provides a summary of the bird species populations that were impacted and the reported causes of their decline.

In some areas of the NY/NJ Harbor Estuary, bird populations are starting to recover. Herring gull, great black-backed gull, heron, egret, and ibis populations have grown since the 1970s. Since the 1980s, the numbers of birds and species diversity has increased dramatically in some areas (Burger *et al.*, 1993; Parsons, 1993). Double-crested cormorants that were noted by Buckley and Buckley (1984) to have disappeared from the Newark Bay region in the early 1900s returned to the area in the late 1980s. Improvements in habitat, coupled with water quality improvements, will be necessary to continue this progress. In particular, the lower portion of the Passaic River has very little viable bird habitat presently available other than intertidal mudflats for foraging.

Other Wildlife

There is very limited information available regarding the wildlife other than aquatic organisms and birds that existed in and

Table 8-3.   Estimated declines in bird production corresponding to
historical wetlands losses in the Newark Bay region

Year	Acres of Wetlands	Estimated Bird Production (adult abundance)[a]	Cumulative Percent Loss
Pre-1816	24,728	3,173	—
1870	18,428	2,365	25.5
1905	15,356	1,971	37.9
1932	12,030	1,544	51.3
1940	11,180	1,435	54.8
1954	8,738	1,121	64.7
1966	5,574	716	77.4
1976	3,570	458	85.6
1989	3,058	393	87.6
1997	2,921	375	88.2

Notes:
[a] Estimate for adult waterbirds that are dependent on coastal wetland habitat
for breeding and foraging. Relationship based on data reported in Custer and
Osborn (1977).

around the Passaic River throughout its history. Large predatory
and game animals were present in the early days of colonization.
The anecdotal information that is available suggests that the area
supported larger populations of the aquatic and semi-aquatic
reptiles, amphibians, and mammals that still occur in the region.

In the late 1600s, bounties were offered in Newark on wolves
that preyed on domestic flocks. Both bears and wolves were present until at least the early 1700s, and a deer was killed by a
hunter in East Orange in 1830. Throughout this period (Pierson, 1917):

"... fur-bearing animals were captured and their pelts used in
making warm garments for the women and children. Wild pigeons,

116

Table 8-4. Summary of impacted bird populations and reported causes of their decline

Species	Cause(s)	Source
American Bittern	Draining of marshes	Urner, 1935; Fables, 1955
American Coot	Draining of marshes	Urner, 1935
Bobolink	Draining of marshes	Urner, 1935
Caspian Tern	Over-hunting	Cruickshank, 1942
Clapper Rail	Draining of marshes	Urner, 1935; Fables, 1955
Common Tern	Over-hunting	Cruickshank, 1942
Ducks	Draining of marshes	Urner, 1935
Dunlin	Over-hunting	Cruickshank, 1942
Eastern Dowitcher	Over-hunting	Cruickshank, 1942
Egret	Millinery trade	Peet and Johnson, 1996
Florida Gallinule	Draining of marshes	Urner, 1935
Forster's Tern	Over-hunting	Cruickshank, 1942
Grasshopper Sparrow	Habitat loss	Fables, 1955
Great Blue Heron	Millinery trade	Peet and Johnson, 1996
Hudsonian Godwit	Habitat loss	Fables, 1955
Laughing Gull	Over-hunting	Cruickshank, 1942
Least Bittern	Draining of marshes	Urner, 1935
Least Tern	Over-hunting	Cruickshank, 1942
Marbled Godwit	Habitat loss	Fables, 1955
Marsh Wren	Habitat loss	Fables, 1955
Migratory Birds	Oil spills	Hurley, 1992
Pectoral Sandpiper	Over-hunting	Cruickshank, 1942
Pied-Billed Grebe	Draining of marshes	Urner, 1935
Piping Plover	Over-hunting	Cruickshank, 1942
Red Knot	Over-hunting	Cruickshank, 1942
Ruddy Turnstone	Over-hunting	Cruickshank, 1942
Seaside Sparrow	Mosquito extermination work	Fables, 1955
Short Eared Owl	Draining of marshes	Cruickshank, 1942
Virginia Rail	Draining of marshes	Urner, 1935; Fables, 1955
Wading Birds	Draining of marshes	Urner, 1935

ducks, and turkeys, flocking about the watering places, furnished the homes with a choice array of edibles."

However, by the mid-1800s, hunters had to travel to the highlands well beyond the city to find game.

According to Charles A. Van Winkle, a Rutherford resident who spent his childhood in the meadowlands in the late 1800s, "The meadows were full of crabs, fish, snapping turtles, muskrats, birds . . . ." Snapping turtles were hunted for their meat. Diamondback terrapins were once nearly extirpated from the meadowlands but are making a comeback. Mud turtles and painted turtles are also found in the meadowlands (Quinn, 1997).

An 1892 article in the *Bloomfield Citizen* newspaper noted that the muskrats that inhabited the area around Silver Lake were driven from their lodges when the lake was drained and the surrounding area cleared (Black and Riggin, 1982). Muskrats were trapped intensively throughout the region for their pelts until the trapping trade was no longer lucrative (Quinn, 1997).

9

FISHING
Where have all the Anglers Gone?

"Urban fishing is a segment of outdoor recreation
that is in urgent need of attention . . . ."

W.F. and J.W. Sigler (1990)

Pre-Civil War Era

In the early to mid-1800s, the Passaic River was "the" freshwater fishing stream in New Jersey (Brydon, 1974). The River was
one of the best shad streams on the East Coast, attracting fishing parties from New York and Brooklyn (Galishoff, 1970). The
River also supported an extraordinary smelt fishery. According
to C.G. Hine in 1909:

"The smelt of the Passaic and Raritan rivers was an entirely differ-
ent fish from that of the Connecticut and more eastern rivers, and
commanded a far higher price in the New York markets . . . The
peculiar cucumber odor, in the freshly caught fish, and the extreme

119

*delicacy of the flesh, both of which are so far superior in the fish of the
Passaic, as to be obvious to the least inquisitive observer."*

Herring, suckers, bass, pickerel, white and yellow perch, sunfish, and sturgeon were also abundant (Galishoff, 1970). Freshwater eels and mussels were very popular (Holmes, 1890; Newark
Athletic Club News, 1921; Brydon, 1974). Crabs and shrimp
were caught in the creeks and inlets (Galishoff, 1970).

Hugh Holmes, a lifelong resident and the first mayor of
Belleville, provided his recollection of fishing on the Passaic
River in the 1820s (Holmes, 1890):

*"You could take a rod and line and in one hour return with your bas-
ket full, as many as you wanted . . . and as far as your eye could
see the whole water would be alive with them from four inches to
two feet in length; bass weighing from one to fifteen pounds."*

Other accounts support Holmes' remarkable descriptions. In
1838, a record sturgeon measuring 5 feet in length and weighing
51 pounds was caught in the Passaic River. This record was bro-
ken 3 weeks later when anglers caught a 7-foot sturgeon that
weighed an estimated 103 pounds (Brydon, 1974). C.G. Hine
recalled "striped bass weighing 66 pounds, sturgeon 6 feet long,
and a host of other fish that swam the Passaic" (Hine, 1909).

Green Island was a popular fishing spot on the Passaic River.
This small island was 50 yards off the west bank in Newark and
measured 33 yards in width by 117 yards in length. Nearby was
a striped bass spawning reef, and shad and smelt fishing were
popular there (Rankin, 1930). The shad and smelt industry was
so well established on Green Island that individuals could rent

120

the rights for a day or week to do their own exclusive fishing (Hine, 1909).

The Beginning of the Decline in Fishing

Figure 9-1 highlights the changes experienced by the Passaic River fishery. The decline in the productivity of this fishery began in the mid-1800s and continued for the next 150 years.

In the mid-1800s, the channel between Green Island and the west bank of the Passaic was filled, and the eastern shore of the island was extended into the River to create additional land. Railroad tracks were later laid on the former fishing spot to connect the Erie line between Newark and Passaic, effectively eliminating this popular fishing site (Hine, 1909).

In 1853, a temporary downturn in the smelt runs occurred when a chain-ferry began operating approximately 1 mile north of the Passaic River's mouth on Newark Bay (Forester, 1854).

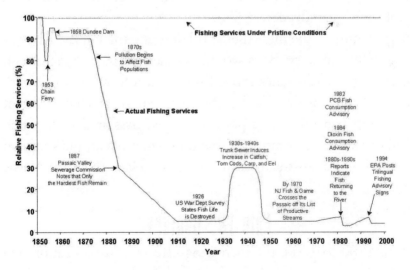

Figure 9-1. History of fishing services in the Passaic River—1850 to present

The ferry's three large chains reached from the east to west bank of the River and were in constant motion. According to an account in 1854 (Forester, 1854):

> *"Since the establishment of this ferry no school of fish, either shad or smelt, has run up the river, though they are still taken below the obstruction, though in diminished numbers."*

The chain-ferry and the filling of Green Island foreshadowed the effects of urbanization and industrialization that would affect fishing and other recreation activities later in the century.

The construction of the Dundee Dam in 1858 ended shad and sturgeon runs that had previously continued as far upriver as the Great Falls (Brydon, 1974). But fish were plentiful above the dam in Dundee Lake and according to Brydon, "The fishing was superb; bass, shad, perch, and many other species abounded and were readily available to those wishing to test their skill with hook and line" (Brydon, 1974).

Accounts in the mid-1860s still describe the Passaic River as an excellent fishery. Boys would net catfish, pike, "roach," and white perch with seines made from mosquito netting (Newark News, 1905). Shrimp and crabs were caught at Center Street Bridge in Newark, and a popular striped bass and white perch fishery was located nearby. At that time, smelt, shad, and sturgeon occured as far upstream as the Dundee Dam (Newark News, 1905).

Late 19th Century

From 1880 to 1900, the increasing effects of urbanization, industrialization, and pollution changed the Passaic River from a recreational stream to a polluted urban waterway (The Board of Education . . . , 1914; Newark Athletic Club News, 1921; Star-Ledger, 1946; White, 1953; Newark News, 1956; Galishoff, 1970; Brydon, 1974; Cawley and Cawley, 1942). As early as 1885, the Commissioner of Fisheries of New Jersey reported adverse impacts on the shad populations of the Passaic River caused by water pollution (Esser, 1982). In 1890, Hugh Holmes noted that:

"Any one looking at the Passaic River between Newark and Passaic in this modern day can hardly imagine what an attractive stream the river used to be."

The 1897 Pollution Report of the Passaic Valley Sewerage Commission states:

"Fish-life, excepting of a few hardy kinds, has disappeared from the river, and 15 years ago shad which formerly frequented the stream abandoned it."

After 1900, conditions remained dire. A 1904 photograph, Figure 9-2, shows a fishing expedition about to cast off a Fourth Street dock in Newark. The caption reads (Newark Evening News, 1934):

"The fisherman go to tend their nets? By no means. They are fishermen, all right, but this trip was undertaken with the idea of eating (that is, picnicking), not catching fish, and it was much more successful, probably than if the latter had been the objective."

Pollution also affected fishing further upstream. Dundee Lake was in decline:

Figure 9-2. Fishermen's expedition casting off from 4th Avenue in Newark—1904 (from the collections of the Newark Public Library).

"But this idyllic scene gradually faded from view as the effects of pollution began to be felt. Industrial wastes from up the river at Paterson increased as that city's manufactories became more numerous. Human wastes made their contribution. The once clear and beautiful lake filled and darkened with debris. The odors became intolerable. The fish disappeared, as did the fishermen and the boatsmen. By 1920, Dundee Lake was considered by some to be a cesspool, unfit for human visitors." (Brydon, 1974)

By 1926, a U.S. War Department survey found "fish life destroyed" in the Passaic River (Hurley, 1992). Municipalities attempted to restore the Passaic River by constructing the trunk sewer, which temporarily improved fishing conditions (McFadden, 1962; Galishoff, 1970; Brydon, 1974). In the 1930s and

1940s, for example, catfish, tom cod, carp, and eels were still fished from the Passaic River (Carr, 1936; Newark News, 1940; Cunningham, 1949). However, the Passaic River fishery did not recover from its initial collapse.

Recent Developments

By 1970, the New Jersey Fish and Game Commission had "given up" on the major sections of the Passaic River. The River's condition was so poor that the commission no longer kept statistics on fish life in the River (Mitchell, 1970). The commission suggested that ". . . the better tributaries (of the Passaic) have not been able to stem the tide of pollution enough to keep the waters suitable for fresh water game fish" (Mitchell, 1970). Bruce Pyle, assistant chief of fisheries management stated:

> *"We haven't done any work in the main sections of the river in a long time . . . We more or less crossed them off the list as productive streams."* (Mitchell, 1970)

Pollution control legislation, improved wastewater treatment, the efforts of local community-action groups, and over $4 billion in cleanup expenses have improved water quality on the Passaic River and expanded opportunities for recreational anglers. Most accounts from the 1980s and 1990s suggest that fishing opportunities have improved from the previous decades.

By 1996, "by all accounts, the Passaic is a lot cleaner today than it was then (10–15 years before)" (Peet and Johnson, 1996). The *Star-Ledger* described the efforts responsible for the turnaround by stating:

"The fishermen say, and environmentalists agree, that after more than $4 billion and thousands of man-hours in cleanup, pollution-sensitive fish like the striped bass are making a comeback, although the state Department of Environmental Protection says the fish still have unsafe levels of dioxin, DDT, and mercury."

Despite gains in water quality and fish numbers, angling levels are likely to remain low along the lower portion of the Passaic River for the foreseeable future. Anglers choose fishing sites for many reasons, not just the number of fish. For the Passaic River specifically, site attributes impacting angler site-choice selection include shoreline modifications constraining River access, poor facilities, high crime or the perception of crime, low aesthetic value, and the largely private (and protected from trespass) nature of the shoreline. Even though fish populations are improving to some degree, these other attributes remain and continue to limit anglers' ability and desire to fish in the Passaic River. Shoreline modifications such as filling in the channel between Green Island and the western shoreline of the River have removed once-popular fishing sites. The construction of the Route 21 Highway in 1965 all but eliminated access to the River's west bank from Northern Newark to the Town of Passaic.

There are only three poorly maintained public boat ramps and docks located from the mouth at Newark Bay to Dundee Dam (Riverbank Park in Kearny, The William Gallagher Recreation Area in Lyndhurst, and the boat ramp at the DeJessa Memorial Bridge). In the lower Passaic River, there are only five potential access points (Riverbank Park in the Ironbound section of Newark, The Newark Heliport [future site of Minish Park], a vacant lot next to the Hess Gas Station on Bridge Street, the bulkhead behind the Pathmark Grocery Store on Passaic Avenue, and Riverbank Park in Kearny). The majority of the shoreline in this section of the River is private property and includes chain link fences, shipping containers, and industrial facilities. This section of the River also passes through the City of Newark, so crime rates or belief in high crime rates is a factor in choosing a fishing location. Therefore, while water quality has improved and the number of fish species in the River has increased, recreational fishing levels are severely limited by River access, facilities available, and aesthetic and safety concerns.

10
ROWING
A Lost Recreational Tradition

"Rowing is more than a fast boat on race day . . . ."

R. Clother (date unknown)

The Golden Era of Rowing

Rowing on the Passaic River traditionally involved shells: "narrow, light racing boats propelled by one or more persons pulling oars or sculls" (Mish, 1994). The Passaic River's "golden era of rowing" (Figure 10-1) began with the formation of the Passaic Boat Club in 1865 and lasted until 1885 (Newark Daily Advertiser, 1866; Newark Athletic Club News, 1921; White, 1953; McFadden, 1962). Other clubs were created in subsequent years including the Nereid, Eureka, Triton, Atlanta, Essex, Institute Boat Club, and the Anneke Jans Club (Star-Ledger, 1929; Falzer, 1947; White, 1953; McFadden, 1962). At one time, eight large boating clubs rowed the Passaic River between Newark

Figure 10-1. Boat races on the Passaic River in Newark—late 1800s (from the collections of the Newark Public Library).

Table 10-1. Passaic River boat clubs

Rowing Club	Founded
Passaic Boat Club	1865
Nereid Boat Club in Newark	1866
Triton Boat Club	1868
Mystic Boat Club	1869
Eureka Boat Club	1873
Nereid Boat Club in Belleville	1875
Passaic River Amateur Rowing Association	1875
Essex Boat Club	1876
Institute Boat Club	1878
Atalantis (sic) Boat Club	1890
Riverside Athletic Club	1890
Newark Rowing Club	1894

Sources: Newark Daily Advertiser, 1866; Van Deventer, 1964.

Bay and Nutley (Newark Athletic Club News, 1921).[2] Table 10-1 lists each boat club in the late 19th century and the year it was founded.

The Passaic River Amateur Rowing Association was formed in 1875 and began organizing large regattas (White, 1953; Brydon, 1974). The first regatta on the Passaic River was in 1876 (Brydon, 1974). It drew nationwide attention, and a national regatta was held on the River in 1878 (Hine, 1909; White, 1953). As many as 5,000 spectators regularly attended the races held twice a year on Memorial Day and the Fourth of July (Newark Athletic Club News, 1921; Michelson, 1932; Falzer, 1947; Mc-Fadden, 1962; Galishoff, 1970). A covered grandstand built above the Erie Railroad bridge held thousands of spectators, and

---

[2] These "boat clubs" were primarily organized as rowing clubs for the sport of crew and are therefore included in the rowing section.

131

others watched from steamers, barges, or other boats (McFadden, 1962; Peet and Johnson, 1996). A *Newark News* (McFadden, 1962) article states:

> *For 20 years before the 1890s opened, boating and other sports (swimming and fishing) flourished on the river. Regattas on Memorial Day and July 4 were high points in the year's social calendar.*

Successful rowers, including the well-known "Eureka Four," rivaled baseball players in popularity (McFadden, 1962; Galishoff, 1970).

Despite increased levels of pollution, rowing remained popular well into the 1880s. A 1929 *Star-Ledger* article stated:

> *In the early [18]80s summer holidays saw the Passaic river in gala decorations. Local boat clubs, with pennants flying from their docks and with large crowds looking on, staged regular meets . . . From noon to twilight the docks and lumber yards along the river would be crowded with enthusiastic rooters.*

Late 19th Century Decline

From 1885 to 1900, rowing in the Passaic River rapidly declined due to urban and industrial pollution (see Figure 10-2). In 1900, sewage and industrial pollution drove rowing from the Passaic River. No regattas were held until 1925 (Hine, 1909; Newark Athletic Club News, 1921; Star-Ledger, 1929; White, 1953; McFadden, 1962; Galishoff, 1970; Brydon, 1974). In 1909, C.G. Hine stated, "It is still a matter of common remark by oarsmen of other localities that the Passaic was the finest river on which they ever rowed" (Hine, 1909). Another account in 1921 from the *Newark Athletic Club News* stated:

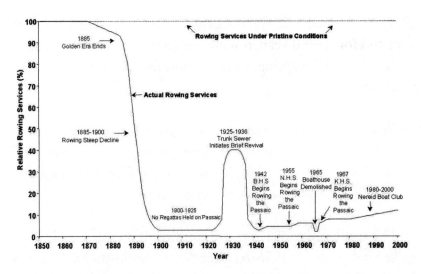

Figure 10-2. History of rowing services on the Passaic River—1850 to present

"Those who did not know it in the days of its cleanliness and whole-someness find it hard to picture the putrid, polluted Passaic River as a place of sport and pleasure. But for 40-odd years it was the scene of aquatic sports which developed oarsmen who carried Newark pennants into the big national regattas."

The same account also describes hopes for the future:

"But there are still many who would like to use the river for motor boating, rowing and canoeing and enough of the old-time members of the almost extinct clubs left to give things a start if the river will only come back to undiluted respectability."

Trunk Sewer Revival

In 1924, the completion of the Passaic Valley trunk sewer bol-stered hopes for River restoration (White, 1953; McFadden,

133

1962). Following a 25-year absence, boat clubs began to reappear, and for several years rowing competitions were held almost weekly during the spring, summer, and fall. A 1929 *Star-Ledger* article stated:

> *"With the purification of the river through completion of the Passaic sewer, however, interest in watersports on the stream is being revived. A new organization, the Passaic River Association, is being permanently organized and old ones are being revived."*

The trunk sewer did improve conditions on the Passaic River for several years. A 1956 *Newark News* article stated, "For two decades there was gradual improvement in the condition of the River" (Newark News, 1956). One *Newark News* account described a Nereid Boat Club rowing regatta as late as September of 1936 (Newark News, 1936b).

But the revival was short-lived. Although water quality improved between 1925 and 1940, rowers encountered frequent dredging activities and heavy commercial shipping traffic. Norman Brydon (1974) wrote:

> *". . . the Army Corps of Engineers began to deepen the river channel and pumped the silt from the bottom to areas along the banks that required filling. The dredges, pumps, and hoses on the river, plus other equipment, made it difficult to conduct races. This activity extended into the period of the depression of the 1930s. One by one the yacht clubs hauled down their flags and went out of existence."*

By the 1940s the trunk sewer was unable to effectively handle the increasing sewage produced by growing population and industry and rowers again abandoned the Passaic (Crawford *et al.*, 1994).

After the brief revival, high-school teams were the only organized rowers on the Passaic River. In 1942, a member of the Nereid Boat Club organized the first high-school rowing team on the Passaic River at Belleville High School. Nutley High School followed years later, and in 1967, Kearny High School began rowing the Passaic River (Metro Newark, 1981). In the 1960s, Nutley and Belleville High Schools maintained regular training on the River. Seventy-five to 100 students from each school rowed from March through June (McFadden, 1962). However, in 1965, the Nutley and Belleville High School boathouse was demolished for construction of the Route 21 Highway (Belleville News, 1969). A new boathouse was dedicated in 1969 and is presently used by Nutley, Belleville, and Kearny High Schools (Belleville News, 1969).

Recent Developments

In the 1980s, the Nereid Boat Club began renovating an old Rutherford boathouse and resumed rowing on the Passaic River. A *Star-Ledger* article from 1996 described the present-day Nereid Boat Club by stating, "Two dozen people are lined up on the dock waiting to get into the water. The Passaic may not be fit to swim in, but it's just fine for their purposes" (Peet and Johnson, 1996). A 30-year-old member said, "It's not nearly as bad as when I was in high school: the debris, the pollution, the odors" (Peet and Johnson, 1996).

The Nereid Boat Club has over 100 members, many of whom travel from Manhattan in the early morning or on weekends (Nereid Boat Club, 1999). The coach and two members described the Passaic as a good river for rowing, explaining that debris affects rowing more than chemical pollution. They encounter logs and miscellaneous debris most frequently, and at least one member has encountered a dead body (Nereid Boat Club, 1999). The coach indicated that the club is actively recruiting novice and expert members, and a *Star-Ledger* article stated that the Nereid Club is proving so popular that some members are worried it is getting too crowded (Passaic River Coalition, 1983; Peet and Johnson, 1996).

Currently, the only rowing organizations on the Passaic River are the Belleville, Nutley, and Kearny high school teams and the revived Nereid Boat Club. Attempts are being made to form a Passaic River Rowing Association (Nereid Boat Club, 1999). However, until the enormous quantity of floatable debris that drifts up and down the lower Passaic with each tide is controlled, the River cannot return to its former state of rowing glory.

11

BOATING
Proud Past, but Little Present

". . . always, in New Jersey, the rivers ruled."

H.E. Wildes (1943)

The 19th Century

The first passenger steamships arrived on the Passaic River in 1838, providing views of the stately homes and broad lawns that bordered the River (Holmes, 1890; Brydon, 1974). Because of the steamships' popularity, boating parties were common on the River (The Board of Education . . . , 1914; Brydon, 1974). Norman Brydon (1974) wrote that "the voices of young people, accompanied by a mandolin or guitar, could be heard across the water." For the next 25 years, people continued to use the steamships for transportation and recreation along the Passaic River.

Descriptions of the period before 1865 suggested that the River was a haven for boating activity. A 1961 *Newark Sunday News* article (Prial, 1961) described the antebellum period:

"The river became a meeting place for fisherman, young people on [boating] outings, and champion rowers and canoeists. On warm summer Sundays, the river was crowded with all kinds of boats . . . Pleasure seekers on the river could moor at delightful inns along the shore in Belleville, Nutley, and Passaic. The inns usually featured German food and beer served out under the trees or on their private docks."

A favorite stop for boaters was Ed Holt's "Floating Palace," an old ship converted into a tavern that was anchored in the middle of the River (Prial, 1961). According to descriptions, boaters would tie up alongside the makeshift tavern, order a drink, and return to the River (Hine, 1909; Prial, 1961). According to C.G. Hine (1909), for a short while there was a second floating tavern anchored at Dead Man's Bend, opposite the lower end of Green Island.

About this time, Coney Island and Rockaway became popular attractions for the citizens of New York, Jersey City, and Newark. Beginning in 1845, Sunday steamboat excursions brought people from Newark to Coney Island:

"Then came the excitement of the trip down the Passaic, across Newark Bay and New York Harbor and by the Statue of Liberty, to the first glimpse of Coney." (Brydon, 1974)

In 1858, the Dundee Dam ended navigation further north but created Dundee Lake, a popular recreation site until the turn of the century. Boating and other watersports flourished on the lake. Regattas were held regularly and canoe, sailboat, and scull races took place throughout the warmer months. Recreation continued on the lake until the early 1900s when pollution impacted the lake's recreation appeal.

In 1862, passenger steamship service began to decline (see Figure 11-1) as horse-car transportation was extended along the Passaic River. In subsequent years, some attempted to revive the declining passenger service, but competition from the horse-car transports and pollution hindered the attempts. The *Passaic Queen* was one of the last steamships to serve the Passaic River, and Norman Brydon (1974) observed that in the 1890s:

"Pollution finally took its toll. At low tide the Passaic was described as worse than an open sewer. The stench was too much for the passengers . . . Gradually, as pollution followed industrialization and the increasing population in cities along the river, pleasure

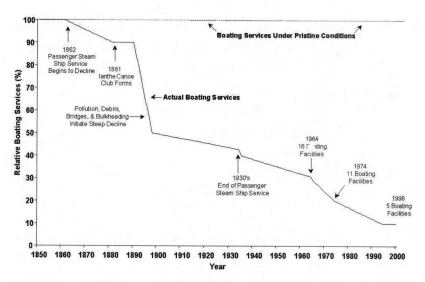

Figure 11-1. History of boating services on the Passaic River—1850 to present

boating along the lower Passaic became only a memory. The excursion boats had left the river as its beautiful estates, farms, and picnic areas had given way to factories and their by-products. Their wastes filled the once green shoreline. Debris piled up along the banks."

Despite pollution, sport canoeing was popular in 1880, and in 1881 the Ianthe Canoe Club was formed. In August of 1882, the Triton Boat Club invited the Ianthe Club to participate in the first canoe race ever held on the River. During the following five years, the Ianthe Club prospered as its members acquired many canoeing titles. The Club remained in existence until the late 19th century, when "the condition of the river drove [the Ianthe and] all boating from its surface" (Hine, 1909).

Early 20ᵗʰ Century

By the turn of the century, the Passaic River was so heavily polluted that a 1902 *Sunday Call* illustration joked about boating on the River (Figure 11-2). The caption under the Christopher Columbus figurehead reads:

"Brave Christopher Columbo, who
Once prowled this side the ocean,
Cruises the foul Passaic now
With visible emotion."

Despite the increasing pollution, yacht clubs along the Passaic River were active in the early 20th century. According to the March 30, 1907 issue of the Amusement News and Weekly Record (McFadden, 1962):

HOW WOULD YOU ENJOY BEING A FIGUREHEAD ON THE POLLUTED PASSAIC?
Ornamental Pieces for the Bows of Vessels Are Coming Into Fashion Again---For the Sake of the Images It
to Be Hoped None of the Craft That Bears Them Will Poke Their Noses Further Up Than Newark Bay.

Figure 11-2. Cartoon joking about boating in the Passaic River (The Sunday Call, 1902).

"Local yachtsmen are busy these days with their craft, getting in readiness for the coming season . . . It is expected that this will be one of the biggest seasons for the boatmen Newark has ever seen."

However, this article also reported that many yachtsmen were planning to go to races elsewhere. It is unclear how much recreational boating was actually done on the Passaic River at that time.

In 1915 the Passaic River Yacht Club opened a new facility on the Hackensack River (Newark News, 1915). An older club, located on the Passaic River in Harrison, remained in use. The club had nearly 400 members and a fleet of 167 boats at both facilities.

Although pollution and competition with horse-car trans-

141

portation had ended passenger steamship service along the Passaic River, steamboat excursions to Coney Island and Rockaway continued. In 1912, advertisements in the *Newark Evening News* for July 1st indicate two lines still serviced Coney Island. The Coney Island and Rockaway boats continued to run until the late 1930s when the Great Depression and World War II ended the service.

A 1938 account described the effect of a storm on pleasure boats moored on the Passaic River. The article stated that "boats were torn from moorings and piled up against drawbridges from Harrison to Rutherford. More than two score were jammed against the Rutherford Avenue Bridge alone" (Newark News, 1938). While the description says little about the specifics of available boating opportunities at the time, it indicates that there was still boating on the River.

Accounts from the 1964 and 1974 New Jersey edition of the Boating Almanac list boating facilities on the Passaic River and Newark Bay (Table 11-1). In 1964, there were 16 boating facilities on the Passaic River and 10 on Newark Bay (including the Passaic River Yacht Club on the lower Hackensack River). By 1974, there were only 11 boating facilities on the Passaic River and 6 on Newark Bay. Currently, there are five facilities on the Passaic River and three on Newark Bay including the Passaic River Yacht Club, indicating that the decline in boating has continued.[3]

Accounts of the area by Fred Van Deventer (1964), author of

---

[3] Besides those listed in the table, current facilities on the Passaic River include the Lyndhurst Boat Launch located in the William T. Gallagher Memorial Recreation Area in Lyndhurst and the DeJessa Memorial Bridge Boat Launch in Belleville.

Table 11-1. Boating facilities on Passaic River and Newark Bay in 1964, 1974, and 1998

Name	Waterbody	Location	Facilities	Listed in 1974	Currently Available
Force Boat Yard	Passaic River	Gregory Ave. Bridge, Wallington, NJ	22 moorings 4 slips	No	No
Favorite Marina	Passaic River	South of Gregory Ave. Bridge, E. Rutherford, NJ	35 slips	Yes	No
Passaic Marine Inc	Passaic River	745 River Drive, Passaic, NJ	22 slips	No	No
Rutherford Marine Service Corp	Passaic River	350 Riverside Ave., Rutherford, NJ	20 moorings 6 docks	No	No
Kurt's Boat Landing	Passaic River	550 Riverside Ave., Rutherford, NJ	30 moorings 30 slips	No	No
Lyndhurst Marine	Passaic River	221 Riverside Ave., Lyndhurst, NJ	50 moorings 50 slips	Yes[a]	No
Pleasure Craft Marine Center	Passaic River	291 River Road, N. Arlington, NJ	12 moorings	Yes	No
W. Hudson District Sea Scout Base	Passaic River	Passaic Ave. Kearny, NJ	[b]	Yes	No
Rapp's Boat Yard	Passaic River	701 Passaic Ave., Kearny, NJ	20 moorings	Yes	Yes
U.S. Coast Guard Aux. Flotilla #305	Passaic River	McCarter Highway, Newark, NJ	[b]	Yes	No
Newark Motor & Yacht Club	Passaic River	McCarter Highway, Newark, NJ	[b]	Yes	No
McConlouge's West Hudson Boat Landing	Passaic River	465 Passaic Avenue, Kearny, NJ	40 moorings	No	No
Smith's Boat Yard	Passaic River	103 Riverside Avenue, Newark, NJ	[b]	Yes	Yes
Kearny Riverbank Park Marina	Passaic River	Passaic Avenue, Kearny, NJ	30' stone ramp	Yes	Yes
City Dock	Passaic River	Newark, NJ	[b]	Yes, but moved	No
"The Boathouse"	Passaic River	191 Blanchard Avenue, Newark, NJ	80 moorings 10 slips	Yes	No
Passaic River Yacht Club	Hackensack River	Lincoln Highway and Hackensack River	[b]	Yes	Yes
Roosevelt Stadium Marina Inc	Newark Bay	Rt. 400, Jersey City, NJ	200 slips	Yes	No
Sheehan's Boat Yard	Newark Bay	Rt. 440, South of Roosevelt Stadium, Bayonne, NJ	100 moorings	No	No
Roanoke Motor & Yacht Club	Newark Bay	Ft. of Doremus Avenue, Newark, NJ	[b]	Yes	No
Jerry's Landing	Newark Bay	51st St, Bayonne, NJ	30 moorings	No	No
south Hudson Boat Club	Newark Bay	51st St, Bayonne, NJ	[b]	No	No
Robbins Reef Yacht Club	Newark Bay	Pavonia Avenue, Bayonne, NJ	[b]	Yes	Yes
Elco Marina	Newark Bay	163 Ave. A Bayonne, NJ	135 slips	Yes	Yes
Jersey Yacht Club	Newark Bay	Bayonne, NJ	[b]	No	No
Singer Yacht Club	Newark Bay	Bayonne, NJ	[b]	Yes	No

Notes:
[a] Lyndhurst Yacht Club added between 1964 and 1974.
[b] Facilities not listed.
Sources: Boating Almanac Co., Inc., 1964; Boating Almanac Co., Inc., 1974.

143

Cruising New Jersey Tidewater: A Boating and Touring Guide, provide insight into the potential reasons for the decline in boating activity and facilities. He stated in the 1964 guide that:

". . . even if you spend only one night in the industrial section of Newark Bay, your boat will be covered by a coat of scum from the oil refineries, belching smokestacks, and industrial waste that is dumped into the rivers and bays . . ."

Besides concern over pollution, boaters had to cope with industrial debris:

"The Coast Guard reports that it handles hundreds of cases every year as the result of small craft being rammed by, or ramming into, the flotsam and jetsam carried into the Upper Bay and Lower Bay. It is not unusual to see old pilings, some of them thirty or forty feet in length, bobbing in the harbor, partially submerged. Large steel ships are unaffected by them, but pleasure craft can be sunk by them."

River congestion increased the danger of boating. A 1966 USACE report stated:

"There is no satisfactory area at the head of Newark Bay which can provide safe and adequate turning space for the large sized ocean going tankers and freighters that enter the Hackensack and Passaic River or discharge their cargo at the oil terminal at the junction of Newark Bay and Passaic Rivers . . . The existence of these conditions is borne out by the record of collisions and accidents which have occurred in the Newark Bay, Hackensack and Passaic Rivers during the 13½-year period from 1950 to June 1963. Of the 59

144

recorded accidents, most were due to groundings and collisions be-
tween vessels, and the balance to collisions with bridges."

Van Deventer summarized the effects of these conditions on boating: "there are very few pleasure boats to be seen" on the Passaic and Hackensack Rivers (Van Deventer, 1964).

Recent Developments

In 1984, the Passaic River Coalition released "A Preliminary Debris Survey of the Lower Passaic River." The debris survey identified over 100 sources of drift and debris, including 6 barges, over 400 pilings, and a half-mile of decaying bulkheads (Passaic River Coalition, 1984). Ella Filippone, Executive Administrator of the Passaic River Coalition, noted that "The debris is dangerous to recreational and commercial boating and is a blight on the river" (Passaic River Coalition, 1984). A *Star-Ledger* article from 1996 stated that the public boat ramps in Nutley, Lyndhurst, and Kearny "are rarely used, and you might have to plow through debris to get your boat in the water" (Peet and Johnson, 1996).

Edward Gertler (1992), in his book *Garden State Canoeing: A Paddler's Guide to New Jersey*, described two canoe routes on the Passaic River in the 1990s. The first route was from Two Bridges, north of Dundee Dam, to the NJ Route 3 Highway. Gertler describes the scenery as "poor to good" and states "though the Passaic is not the sewer it once was, water quality still becomes detectably worse than above [Paterson]." He continued:

"The remaining miles [from Passaic to Route 3] are through both
industrial and residential neighborhoods. The banks are incredibly
trashy. Access is minimal as many of the riverside parks are fenced

off on their waterfront side. This being commercially navigable water, most of the bridges on this reach are drawbridges."

The second canoeing route discussed by Gertler was from Route 3 to the mouth of the Passaic River at Newark Bay. He rated this 11-mile stretch of the River as "fair to ugly" and described it:

"Initially there are a few riverside parks to soften the scenery. The skyline of Newark and the vertical-lift drawbridges are interesting. Once past Newark though, the river enters a world of freeways, railroads, factories, and chemical plants. Approaching the mouth, the sickening smell of solvents permeates the air."

Several factors continue to limit recreational boating on the Passaic River. The Route 21 Highway from Newark to Passaic reduces access to the west bank (Community Planning Associates, 1972). Analysis of Sanborn Maps of Newark from 1950 to 1989 shows that the highway replaced two yacht clubs (including one boat yard) and approximately 200 yards of wooded riverbank between Newark and the southern part of Belleville (Farley, 1999). Dredging, shoreline modification, commercial shipping traffic, and bridge construction limit recreational boating by impairing transit and increasing River congestion.

Bridges in particular (Table 6-1) limit navigation. Although some have ample vertical clearance, several bridges are extremely low (U.S. Coast Guard Bridge Administration, 1984; U.S. Department of Commerce, 1990). While many of these are swing bridges, they are not operated full-time. To open a bridge, a boater must call the owner hours or even days in advance to request that a bridge operator be present (U.S. Coast Guard Bridge Administration, 1997; Rapp, 1998). Boaters who pass a bridge in the morning may be trapped behind the bridge in the afternoon. Today, it is difficult for recreational or commercial boats to navigate the River.

12

SWIMMING
Only a Distant Memory

"How incomplete would be the life of any normal village or country bred boy without the veritable fountain of youth, immortalized in song and story, the old swimming hole."

E.S. Rankin (1930)

BEFORE THE 1870S, THE PASSAIC RIVER attracted swimmers in the summer months. Piers were popular diving spots, and in 1864 swimmers could see the bottom of the "crystal clear" River at a depth of 10 to 13 feet (Newark Athletic Club News, 1921; Galishoff, 1970). However, urbanization, industrialization, and pollution beginning in the late 1800s diminished swimming opportunities, as shown in Figure 12-1.

Swimming accounts are elusive for much of the early 20th century. There was apparently not much swimming in the River between 1875 and 1920. There are numerous accounts of swimming in the 1930s that coincide with the establishment of the

Figure 12-1. Swimming in the Passaic River—post-industrialized conditions (from the collections of the Newark Public Library).

trunk sewer. A *Newark News* article from May of 1933 described swimmers attempting to cool off in the Passaic River (Newark News, 1933a):

> *"There will be plenty of swimming in the Passaic River if yesterday's indications mean anything. Warm weather is bringing the youngsters out in droves to try the old swimming places . . . At Byrne's Beach in the Ironbound section there are life guards and the crowd is largest. A spring board and sandy beach make swimming attractive."*

One month later, in June of 1933, Belleville officials tested the quality of the Passaic River's water to be sure it was safe for swimming. The *Newark News* (1933b) stated:

> *"Adults will be pleased to know that an authoritative analysis reported today for benefits of Belleville residents has it that the river has a clean bill of health for bathing purposes again . . . Neither specimen of river water shows either typhoid germs or any evidence of fecal contamination. There are large numbers of microscopic animals such as are found in swamp water, but such organisms are not harmful to the human body."*

In July of 1936 a summer heat wave brought youngsters to the Passaic River. The *Newark News* (1936a) described the situation:

> *"There were plenty of 'unofficial' dips taken, too, especially by the youngsters. Patronage of the Passaic River was heavy with lookouts posted to spot the approach of the 'law.' The evening showers brought out squads of children in bathing suits to take advantage of the natural shower bath."*

This quote suggests that swimming may have been officially banned in some way as indicated by "lookouts posted to spot the approach of the 'law.'" Figure 12-2 shows a boy diving from a dock into the River. The caption reads: "Older than the city itself is the *now-forbidden* sport of swimming in the Passaic. Here at 'Burns Beach' near Jackson Street, a lad dives 20 feet into 4 feet of water" (The Sunday Call, 1936) (emphasis added).

Children were not the only ones swimming illegally in the River. In September of 1936 a Polar Bear Club had its first meet-

Figure 12-2.   Boy diving into the Passaic River (The Sunday Call, 1936).

ing on the banks of the Passaic River in Nutley. According to accounts (Newark News, 1936c):

> *"Residents from Lyndhurst, across the river, and those living on the*
> *Nutley side reported to police that four or five nudists went swim-*
> *ming yesterday. The group, all men, had departed when police ar-*
> *rived."*

In 1938, nine drowning deaths were reported in the Newark
section of the Passaic River, and new warnings emerged that the
water was contaminated with "deadly" bacteria (Star-Ledger,
1939; Newark News, 1948). In 1939, an official river patrol was
instituted to reduce the number of drownings, guard against
crime along the waterfront, disperse swimming parties, and

watch for other violations (Star-Ledger, 1939). According to a 1939 *Star Ledger* article, swimming persisted in the Newark section of the Passaic River "despite repeated warnings from Health Officer Craster of the dangers to swimmers from contamination and pollution of the stream. It is reportedly infested with deadly germs" (Star-Ledger, 1939).

In 1946, residents along the River protested that the Passaic Valley Sewerage Commission was not keeping the Passaic River clean enough for swimming. The sewerage commission had surveyed the water at nine places between Paterson and the mouth of the River and found that the water was unfit for swimming or drinking. The sewerage commission further concluded that the River would never be fit for swimming or drinking. Ralph Van Duyney, Chief Engineer of the Passaic Valley Sewerage Commission, stated that (Newark News, 1946):

> *"Surface drainage alone from an area as highly settled and industrialized as the Passaic Valley would put too many bacteria into the river for safety . . . and since the trunk sewer was installed, every heavy rainstorm throws such a load of water into the system that downstream sewers must bypass the trunk and empty directly into the river, unless they are to flood the system."*

In 1948, conditions had not improved. A *Newark News* (1948) article stated:

> *"It has been many years since children were allowed to swim off Center Street dock in Newark, although a few courageous and careless youth still chance it. But the floating logs, oil slicks, raw sewage and general pollution have obliterated the river's appeal for swimmers."*

By 1970, conditions even further up the River had not changed. Bob Mitchell (1970), a reporter for the *Newark Sunday News*, recalled:

"As a youth, [I] learned to swim in an 'old swimming hole' in the Passaic River's upper basin. [I] recall the clear waters rippling over pebbled bottoms, making lessons in underwater swimming pleasurably easy. [I] remember vividly, the sandbar, the tree that anchored the traditional swimming rope, and the cornfields that served as impromptu dressing rooms. That was 30 years ago. The sandbar is gone. So is the tree. The cornfields are housing developments. The basin waters now carry a greenish hue, and the river itself is murky and smelly. The waters no longer are inviting, and police chase strangers who think otherwise."

Figure 12-3 provides a historical summary of swimming services in the Passaic River. Even with the improvements in water quality in the River over the past 30 years, there has been no swimming revival. Several factors contribute to swimming remaining virtually nonexistent. First, water quality requirements for swimming are higher than for fishing, boating, and other non-contact recreational uses. The present water quality levels, while improved, do not meet this higher standard. Moreover, as with fishing, many factors beyond water quality contribute to the attractiveness of a site for swimming. For example, the access issues that limit fishing along the Passaic also limit its accessibility for swimming. The area does not have the same picturesque aesthetics that it did when swimming was popular in the mid-19th century. While commercial shipping has declined in the area, its presence is incompatible with recreational swimming,

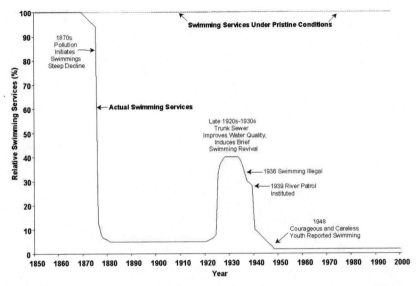

Figure 12-3. History of swimming services in the Passaic River—1850 to present

making it dangerous in some places. And, substitute swimming sites, including man-made swimming pools, have proliferated with the growth in population. Overall, therefore, water quality is only one factor in the elimination of swimming from the Passaic. It may be that even if the water quality increases to a level that would support swimming, people would still not choose to swim there or be able to in any case because of aesthetic factors. In any case, the lower Passaic River is not likely to support swimming for the forseeable future.

155

13

PASSIVE RECREATION
Shrinking Open Space

"Life was gay along the rivers."

H.E. Wildes (1943)

THE ACTIVITIES DESCRIBED IN Chapters 8 through 11 are examples of "active" recreation that has taken place on the Passaic River. The Passaic River also provided passive forms of recreation, including walking along the riverbank, picnicking, and enjoying the view of the River (see Figures 4-7 and 4-8). These passive recreation activities require open space along the River, such as grassy or wooded areas. While there are parks providing such open space today, in the past people enjoyed large open spaces along the River's banks.

The banks of the Passaic River were once lined with farms, trees, inns, estates, and picnic areas (Prial, 1961; Cavnar, 1968; Brydon, 1974). After the Civil War the Passaic was a ". . . pic-

157

nicking paradise, even through the Belleville-Newark area on its way to Newark Bay . . ." (Cavnar, 1968). Large estates were popular gathering places along the River's banks until the latter part of the 19th century. A Newark Athletic News (1921) article stated:

> *"Before the Civil War the banks of the Passaic were lined with proud estates, the ruins of which are apparent now along the river roads on both sides. The families who made their homes there used the river considerably and social intimacy was maintained by intervisiting by way of the water."*

These estates were lined with trees, had lawns stretching down to the River's banks, and were "fitted out with croquet sets and vine-covered pagodas" (McFadden, 1962).

Located on Mt. Pleasant Avenue in Newark, one 17-acre estate included Cockloft Hall (the estate house), a summerhouse, and a pond. Washington Irving visited the estate often and refers to it in his Salmagundi Papers. In a letter to the New Jersey Historical Society he wrote, "With Newark are associated in my mind many pleasant recollections of early days, and of social meetings at an old mansion on the banks of the Passaic." By the 1880s the original 17-acre estate had been reduced as smaller lots were created to accommodate population growth (Shaw, 1884). Presently City Dock #3 and a Conrail bridge occupy this section of the Passaic River's banks (Map of Essex County, 1997).

Around the 1860s, there was a private park on the Passaic River near the mouth of Second River. According to one visitor (Newark News, 1905), the park:

". . . *was in a grove of hemlocks, spruces, oaks and chestnuts, ris-ing abruptly from the river to a height of more than fifty feet . . . [Eilshemius] built rustic stairways about the trunks of some of the big trees, with Summer houses amid the boughs, constructed fences, pathways and stairways of cedar boughs and logs and made the place a veritable garden of natural beauty with ferns, rhododen-drons and vines.*"

The park contained a wharf famous for catching sunfish, cat-fish, yellow perch, and eels. Although technically trespassing when playing in the park, the visitor did not remember ever being chased away. By 1905 there were only traces of the park left. Public sites included locations such as Bird's Woods on the south shore of Second River. Bird's Woods was a popular picnic ground that contained an array of old pines, hemlocks, laurel, partridge berries, and ruins of old mills (Hine, 1909).

Since the 1920s there has been a need for more public parks on the banks of the lower Passaic River. A 1929 article (Star-Ledger, 1929) mentioned the formation of the Passaic River As-sociation, which had as one of its goals the development of park-ways along the banks of the Passaic River. The lack of parkland was consistent with the lack of open space in the surrounding area. In the 1930s, there was an open space deficiency of 10,000 acres for lower Bergen County, Hudson County, and Newark based on a standard of 10 acres per 1,000 people (New Jersey State Planning Board, 1939).

In the 1980s, the Passaic River Restoration Plan, established by the Passaic River Coalition and various municipalities along the lower portion of the Passaic River, focused attention on the need for open space along the River. The main feature of the project is a recreational corridor, which would extend along the east bank of the Passaic River from Rutherford through Kearny. The corridor would include a multi-purpose trail along the edge of the River with "pocket parks," marinas, and other recreational facilities located at various points along the trail (Passaic River Coalition, 1987). While some of the corridor has been created, the Passaic River Coalition and participating municipalities continue to add additional parkland.

The reduction of passive recreation along the Passaic River is linked to multiple factors related to urbanization and industrialization, including the destruction of shoreline habitat, sewage and contaminant releases, debris, and the lack of recreational amenities (Figure 13-1). Each of these factors needs to be considered in order to develop appropriate plans for the re-vitalization of recreation on the River.

Figure 13-1.   View of the Passaic River from Newark—1905 (from the collections of the Newark Public Library).

14

THE PASSAIC RIVER
Moving Forward or Repeating History?

"Most of our environmental problems are the results of our own human behavior; it follows that we are not going to solve these problems until we stop behaving in a manner that causes them."

D.G. Kozlovsky (1974)

THE PASSAIC RIVER, ITS ECOSYSTEMS and services, have declined enormously over the past 300 years. Yet, this decline has not been at a constant or uninterrupted pace. Instead, there have been times of slow degradation, sharp decline, and some improvement. By understanding the history of natural resource losses, the management actions that have failed, and those actions that have at least partially succeeded, we can face the future with greater hope. By building the future on what we learn from the past, we can speed the River's recovery.

163

The Passaic is not unique in its battle with industrialization and urbanization (e.g., MacFarquhar, 1995). Throughout the world, urban river management is a struggle to reverse the tide of ecological history in the context of present-day economics and human population levels. To manage the Passaic River effectively, we need to know what has worked and not worked elsewhere. At the same time, if we do succeed on the Passaic, we will have a model for others to follow.

Much of what was known about urban impacts and urban environmental management in Europe through the mid-1960s is summarized in a single symposium volume: Ecology and the Industrial Society (Goodman *et al.*, 1965). This work includes hopeful lessons in restoration based on the carefully documented impacts to urban lands and waterways. An interesting informational update is available in the *Urban Ecology Annotated Bibliography* (Downton and Munn, 1996), which covers a broad range of sources, both popular and scientific. In the U.S., *Nature's Services: Societal Dependence on Natural Ecosystems* (Daily, 1997) documents the ecological functions of healthy environments. In addition, it points the way to effective restoration by documenting the value of specific ecosystem components. Similarly, Platt *et al.* (1994) illustrate both the value of and restoration approaches for urban biodiversity.

There are many texts available on urban land use and the level of ecological services under various watershed management configurations (for early examples [Hawley, 1971; Havlick, 1974]; for more up-to-date discussion [Calthorpe, 1993]). One of the most important is *The Urban Ecosystem: A Holistic Perspective*, edited by Forrest Stearns and Tom Montag (1974). This book gives a fresh concept for its time, presenting the idea of establishing specific, service-based goals and objectives for urban ecosystem management. This idea acknowledges that humans are now effectively managing the biosphere in general and urban ecosystems in particular. In specific urban settings such as the Passaic River basin, the social history and economics have a tight grip on the landscape. We do not have the option to implement wholesale return of the land to wilderness in the hope that some natural level of services would flow from such an ecosystem. Rather, we must manage a watershed and its component ecosystems in a vital, urban environment, where humans set goals for ecosystems and establish practices to achieve those goals. In an area like the Passaic River, we no longer have the option of managing by default. Instead, we must affirmatively set and meet environmental service objectives (Ludwig, 1985; Ludwig, 1989).

The historical ecology exercise presented in the previous 13 chapters can help provide scientifically sound and technically tractable foundations for establishing and meeting ecosystem service objectives. We undertook this exercise to document the ecological history of the Passaic River, in order to provide a foundation for assessing incremental impacts from the various factors that have caused the River's degradation, and to evaluate management alternatives for moving forward and improving environmental conditions. While it is beyond the scope of our effort here to develop specific management recommendations, we can formulate our findings in a way that facilitates management decision making.

A review of how the Passaic River ecosystem declined can serve as a basis for a discussion of restoring it. From 1996 through 1998, a local reporter for the Newark *Star-Ledger*, C.F. Cummings, published a series of articles that chronicled the troubled history of the Passaic and an optimism for the future (Cummings, 1996a,b; 1997a,b; 1998a,b,c). It is our hope that this book will provide both a detailed understanding of past mistakes and mismanagement of the River, as well as a foundation of hope and potential for future management of its recovering resources.

Prior to European settlement, the watershed faced little human impact because the local Native Americans did not practice widescale burning or other environmental modifications. In the first century of colonization, the watershed was disturbed by clearing and transition from forest to agriculture. Downstream water quality suffered and some biodiversity was lost, although the degree of impact was relatively low. Then came the urbanization of the area in the 1800s. The River was dammed, the cities grew, and the industrial revolution claimed much of the River's flow and its riparian support systems. In this period, sewage drove oxygen levels in the water to levels too low to support life throughout the River. In addition, industrial toxicants from metals processing, petroleum refining, tanning, and other processes were present at high concentrations. In ensuing years, sewage controls gave the River some respite, and there was some ecological recovery. But population growth took the remaining wetlands and tributaries that had once supported the River. Today, the Passaic River is healthier than it has been for a century, but innovative management is needed for further progress.

Because ecosystems are hierarchical structures where processes at higher levels define those at lower levels (Allen and Starr, 1982), the greatest ecological value can be wrung from managing those high level parameters. For example, many aspects of resource services are effected by the loss of broad riparian wetlands and tributaries to the River. If we could restore

166

these aspects of the landscape, we would consequently restore many services, including stormwater retention, pollution abatement, habitat provision, and aesthetic quality. However, in the densely populated Passaic watershed, these high level components are difficult, if not impossible, to restore. Areas that were once thriving wetlands have long since been drained, filled, and developed. A complete reversal of that process is simply not feasible.

Management efforts in the lower levels in the ecosystem hierarchy are more tractable. Currently, the River's banks and shorelines generally lack the sloping, diverse-bottomed habitat that would support correspondingly diverse fish and wildlife populations. Whatever habitat does exist is struggling against the damaging effects of flotsam and debris. If shallow areas could be altered to incorporate wetlands and reefs, backed by shrub or woodland habitat, substantial improvements in biodiversity and fish and wildlife population levels would be expected. Flotsam control would be necessary to establish ecologically functional shorelines.

Habitat improvement would, in turn, support the return of fish and wildlife populations. The services provided by these populations, both human-use and ecological services, would improve as well. For example, increases in fish populations should increase the population of birds who use the fish as a food source. We would also expect that increases in fish populations would lead to an increase in fishing activity. Nevertheless, it is important to remember that even with improved riparian habitat, the Passaic River will remain an urban waterway. Fish population is only one factor in how people choose fishing sites. Access, aesthetics, amenities, and the existence of substitutes will remain important to anglers and will constrain angler activity in response to improved catch rates.

To the degree that fishing services are improved, then the presence of any remaining fish advisories could become a real service impairment. Currently, the fish advisories do not have much effect on angler behavior simply because there is not very much angling activity. But a more functional ecosystem, with healthy shallows and riparian corridors, could sequester and process more chemical inputs, thereby reducing the levels of contaminants found in the fish. Fish advisories might become a thing of the past if sufficient habitat restoration could be undertaken.

Other human use services, such as rowing, boating and passive use services would also benefit from flotsam control and habitat improvements. As with fishing, however, other aspects of the Passaic River will affect recreators' demand of sites in this area. For example, habitat improvement will not change the problem boaters have with low bridges.

In summary, a key step in achieving restoration goals for the Passaic River is setting rational goals. We must remember the long history of development that left the River in its current condition. Although it may be expedient and convenient to blame all of the watershed's ills on the release of industrial contaminants or any other specific activity, our detailed ecological history clearly shows otherwise. The Passaic must be viewed as an urban river in an industrial corridor, and it must be managed with that baseline as a reference. With reasonable restoration goals and diligent planning, the Passaic could well become a model urban river; striking as effective a balance between natural and built environments as its history will allow.

LITERATURE CITED

Abbott CG. 1907. Summer bird-life of the Newark, New Jersey, marshes. *Auk* 24:1–11.

Able KW, Witting DA, McBride RS, Rountree RA, Smith KJ. 1996. Fishes of polyhaline estuarine shores in Great Bay-Little Egg Harbor, New Jersey: a case study of seasonal and habitat influences, p. 335–353. In: Nordstrom KF, Roman CT, editors. *Estuarine shores: Evolution, environments and human alternations.* New York: John Wiley & Sons.

Allen TFH, Starr TB. 1982. *Hierarchy.* Chicago, IL: University of Chicago Press.

Allen TB, Barrett W, Fishbein SL, Kopper P, Lanouette E, Robinson DF, Selim RD, Tourtellot JB. 1987. *Field guide to the birds of North America.* Washington, DC: National Geographic Society.

Atkinson J. 1878. *The history of Newark.* Newark: W.B. Guild.

Ayres RU, Rod SR. 1986. Patterns of pollution in the Hudson-Raritan basin. *Environment* 28(4):14–43.

Barrett N. 1990a. *A bibliography of the habitats and wildlife within the vicinity of the New York/New Jersey Harbor Estuary* [An appendix to the report by Squires and Barclay]. University of Connecticut.

Barrett N. 1990b. *The influence of urban structure and human settlement on birdlife in the New York/New Jersey Harbor Estuary area* [Appendix E to the report by Squires and Barclay]. University of Connecticut.

Beale DT. 1972. *Pollution control on the Passaic River.* A Report of the Center for Analysis of Public Issues.

Belleville News. 1969. Dedication ceremonies planned for boathouse. *Belleville News* 1969 Mar 20.

Bent AC. 1919. *Life histories of North American diving birds.* New York: Dover Publications, Inc.

Bent AC. 1927. *Life histories of North American shore birds, Part I.* New York: Dover Publications, Inc.

Bent AC. 1929. *Life histories of North American shore birds, Part II.* New York: Dover Publications, Inc.

Bent AC. 1938. *Life histories of North American birds of prey. Part 2: orders Falconiformes and Strigiformes*, p. 170–173, p. 176–179. Washington, DC: U.S. Government Printing Office.

Berger J. 1992. The Hackensack River meadowlands, p. 510–518. In *Restoration of aquatic ecosystems: science, technology, and public policy.* Washington, DC: National Academy Press.

Berkes F. 1999. *Sacred ecology: traditional ecological knowledge and resource management.* Philadelphia: Taylor & Francis.

Black S, Riggin MA, editors. 1982. Excerpts from early Bloomfield, N.J. Newspapers 1872–1895, paragraph from *The Bloomfield Citizen*, November 19, 1892. Re: The draining of Silver Lake. Bloomfield (NJ): Historical Society of Bloomfield, NJ.

Board of Public Improvements Topographical Bureau. 1997. General map of the City of New York, Boroughs of Manhattan, Brooklyn, Bronx, Queens and Richmond. New York; 1800. Reprinted in: Cohen PE, Augustyn RT. *Manhattan in maps, 1527–1995.* New York: Rizzoli International Publications, Inc.

Boating Almanac Co., Inc. 1964. *Boating almanac, New Jersey edition.*

Boating Almanac Co., Inc. 1974. *Boating almanac, Vol. 3, New Jersey edition.*

Bone K (editor). 1997. *The New York waterfront: evolution and building culture of the port and harbor.* New York: The Monacelli Press.

Bonnevie NL, Gunster DG, Wenning RJ. 1992. Lead contamination in surficial sediments from Newark Bay, New Jersey. *Environment International* 18: 497–405.

Bonnevie NL, Wenning RJ, Huntley SL, Bedbury H. 1993. Distribution of inorganic compounds in sediments from three waterways in northern New Jersey. *Bull. Environ. Contam. Toxicol.* 51:672–680.

Bonnevie NL, Huntley SL, Found BW, Wenning RJ. 1994. Trace metal contamination in surficial sediments from Newark Bay, New Jersey. *Sci. Total Environ.* 144:1–16.

Bonnicksen TM. 2000. *America's ancient forests: from the ice age to the age of discovery.* New York: John Wiley & Sons, Inc.

Bopp RF, Simpson HJ. 1991. *Sediment sampling and radionuclide and chlorinated hydrocarbon analysis in Newark Bay and the Hackensack and Passaic Rivers: Final report to the State of New Jersey Department of Environmental Protection, Division of Science and Research.* Palisades, NY: Lamont-Doherty Geological Observatory of Columbia University.

Boughey AS. 1971. *Fundamental ecology.* Intext series in ecology. San Francisco: Intext Educational Publishers.

Boyle RH. 1969. *The Hudson River: a natural and unnatural history.* First ed. New York: W.W. Norton & Company, Inc.

Britton NL. 1889. *Catalogue of plants found in New Jersey.* Geological Survey New Jersey Final Report 2:25–642.

Brodhead JR. 1953. *History of the state of New York (microform).* New York: Harper & Brothers.

Brown JJ. 1857. *The American angler's guide.* New York: D. Appleton and Company.

Brydon NF. 1968. New Jersey wildlife conservation and the law. *New Jersey History* 86(4):215–235.

Brydon N. 1974. *The Passaic River: past, present, and future.* New Brunswick (NJ): Rutgers University Press.

Buckley PA, Buckley FG. 1984. Expanding double-crested cormorant and laughing gull populations on Long Island, NY. *The Kingbird* 34:146–155.

Burger J, editor. 1994. *Before and after an oil spill: the Arthur Kill.* New Brunswick (NJ): Rutgers University Press.

Burger J, Parsons K, Gochfeld M. 1993. *Avian populations and environmental degradation in an urban river: the Kills of New York and New Jersey* [Unpublished report].

Calthorpe P. 1993. *The next American metropolis.* Princeton: Princeton Architectural Press.

Carr GB. 1936. River trip industrial index of Newark: Passaic, turned salty, unfolds half-billion dollar panorama. *Sunday Call* 1936 Nov 1.

Cavnar J. 1968. North Jersey waterway. *Newark Sunday News* 1968 June 9; p 6–12.

Cawley J, Cawley M. 1942. *Exploring the little rivers of New Jersey.* New Brunswick (NJ): Rutgers University Press.

Cerrato RM. 1986. *The benthic fauna of Newark Bay.* Stony Brook: Marine Sciences Research Center, State University of New York.

Chapman FM. 1906. The birds of the vicinity of New York City. *American Museum Journal* 6:81–102.

Clother R. Date unkown. Quote available from: Museophile via the INTERNET at http://archive.museophile.sbu.ac.uk/rowing/quotes.html. Accessed Aug. 30, 2001.

Coase R. 1960. The Problem of Social Cost. *Journal of Law and Economics* 3: 1–44.

Cohen PE, Augustyn RT. 1997. *Manhattan in maps, 1527-1995.* New York: Rizzoli International Publications, Inc.

Community Planning Associates. 1972. *Route 21 Newark planning report. A proposal to the New Jersey State Department of Transportation by the City of Newark.* 1972 Feb, NY.

Cook GH, Vermeule CC. 1890. *A topographical map of the valley of the Passaic based on the triangulation of the U.S. Coast and Geodetic Survey.*

Crawford DW, Bonnevie NL, Gillia CA, Wenning RJ. 1994. Historical changes in the ecological health of the Newark Bay Estuary, New Jersey. *Ecotoxicol. Environ. Safety* 29:276–303.

Crawford DW, Bonnevie NL, Wenning RJ. 1995. Sources of pollution and sediment contamination in Newark Bay, New Jersey. *Ecotoxicol. Environ. Safety* 30:85–100.

Cronon W. 1983. *Changes in the land: indians, colonists, and the ecology of New England.* New York: Hill and Wang.

Crosby AW Jr. 1972. *The Colombian exchange: biological and cultural consquences of 1492.* Westport, CT: Greenwood Press.

Crosby AW Jr. 1986. *Ecological imperialism: the biological expansion of Europe, 900–1900.* New York: Cambridge University Press.

Cruickshank AD. 1942. *Birds around New York City: where and when to find them.* New York.

Cummings C. 1996a. New chapter opens in life of the Passaic. *Newark Star-Ledger* 1996 Oct 31.

Cummings CF. 1996b. The lay of the land, from barren beginnings to the most densely populated. *Newark Star-Ledger* 1996 Oct 24.

Cummings CF. 1997a. Passaic lighthouse safeguarded 6 decades of Newark Bay shipping. *Newark Star-Ledger* 1997 Apr 17.

Cummings CF. 1997b. Woodside in the last century: a land rich in game and legend. *Newark Star-Ledger* 1997 Jan 23.

Cummings CF. 1998a. From whalers to warships, always a city of seafarers. *Newark Star-Ledger* 1998 Dec 31.

Cummings CF. 1998b. Once-sweet, now-fouled, Passaic awaits a grand rebirth with park. *The Star-Ledger* 1998 July 9.

Cummings CF. 1998c. Transportation: the magic carpet that whisked in industry. *Newark Star-Ledger* 1998 June 18.

Cunningham JT. 1949. Let's explore—The Passaic's lowlands. *Newark Sunday News* 1949 Sep 4.

Cunningham JT. 1951. Across the meadows: Newark and Paterson among first municipalities to seek charters for railroads as outlets for products. In: Railroading in New Jersey: A series of 17 articles. *The Newark Sunday News* 1951 Jan 7 to Apr 29. New York: Associated Railroads of New Jersey; 12–16.

Cunningham JT. 1954. *Made in New Jersey: the industrial story of a state.* New Brunswick: Rutgers University Press.

Cunningham JT. 1966. *New Jersey: America's main road.* Garden City (NJ): Doubleday & Company, Inc.

Cunningham, J. 1988. *Newark.* Newark: New Jersey Historical Society.

Cunningham JT. 1994. *This is New Jersey.* Fourth ed. New Brunswick: Rutgers University Press.

Custer TW, Osborn RG. 1977. *Wading birds as biological indicators: 1975 colony survey,* p. 28. Washington, DC: U.S. Fish and Wildlife Service.

Dahl TE, Johnson CE, Frayer WE. 1990. *Wetlands status and trends in the conterminous United States mid-1970s to mid-1980s.* U.S. Fish and Wildlife Services, Washington, DC.

Daily GC. 1997. *Nature's services: societal dependence on natural ecosystems.* Washington DC: Island Press.

Day JW Jr., Hall CA, Kemp WM, Y·Òez-Arancibia A. 1989. *Estuarine ecology.* New York: John Wiley.

Diaz RJ, Rosenberg R. 1995. Marine benthic hypoxia: a review of its ecological effects and the behavioural responese of benthic macrofauna. *Oceanogr. Mar. Biol.* 33:245–303.

Downton PF, Munn D, editors. 1996. *Urban ecology annotated bibliography.* Adelaide [Aus]: Centre for Urban Ecology.

Dutcher W. 1886. Destruction of bird-life in the vicinity of New York. *Science [Reprinted from AOU Committee on Protection of Birds Bulletin 1886 1:7–9]* 12(160):197–199.

Earll RE. 1887. New Jersey and its fisheries. Part VII, p. 379–400. In Goode GB, editor. *The fisheries and fishery industries of the United States, Section II: a geographical review of the fisheries industries and fishing communities for the year 1880.* Washington DC: Government Publishing Office.

Ehrlich PR, Dobkin DS, Wheye D. 1988. *The birder's handbook, a field guide to the natural history of North American birds.* New York: Simon and Schuster.

Eisenberg E. 1998. *The ecology of Eden.* New York: Alfred A. Knopf.

Elson T. Killam Associates, Inc. 1976. *Report upon overflow analysis to Passaic Valley Sewerage Commissioners, Passaic River overflows.* Prepared by Elson T. Killam Associates, Inc., Millburn, NJ.

Esselborn W. 1958. *Newark, city of surprises. Its Americana, river, and Down Neck.* Montclair (NJ): Montclair Business Service.

Esser SC. 1982. Long-term changes in some finfishes of the Hudson-Raritan estuary, p. 299–314.. In: Mayer GF, editor. *Ecological stress and the New York bight: science and management.* Rockville (MD): National Oceanic and Atmospheric Administration.

Fables DJ. 1955. *Annotated list of New Jersey birds.* Urner Ornithological Club.

Falzer GA. 1947. End of a Newark era: Passing of institute boat club recalls rowing glory. *Newark Sunday News* 1947 February 16.

Literature Cited

Farley D. 1999. Analysis of 1947 and 1974 aerial photographs and Sanborn Maps 450, 452, 467, and 468. Analysis performed by EI Group, Inc.

Festa P, Toth SJ. 1976. Marshes, mudflats and industry: conservation activities in the estuaries of metropolitan New Jersey. *New Jersey Outdoors* 3(4):6–8.

Fidelity Trust Company. 1916. *Historic Newark: a collection of the facts and traditions abou the most interesting sites, streets and buildings of the city.* First ed. Boston, MA: Walton Advertising & Printing Company.

Finley B, Wenning RJ, Ungs MJ, Huntley S, Paustenbach DJ. 1990. PCDDs and PCDFs in surficial sediments from the lower Passaic River and Newark Bay, p. 409–414. In: Short papers from the 10th International Meeting, Dioxin 90, Volume 1.

Folsom JF. 1900. On the Second River in the good old days. *Newark Evening News*, June 2.

Forester F. 1854. Memoir on the smelt of the Passaic River. *Grahams Magazine* 1854 Oct.

Galishoff S. 1970. The Passaic Valley trunk sewer. *New Jersey History* (The New Jersey Historical Society) Winter 1970: vol. LXXXVIII, no. 4, whole no. 343.

Galishoff S. 1988. *Newark: The nation's unhealthiest city 1832–1895.* New Brunswick [NJ], Rutgers University Press.

Geological Survey of New Jersey. 1899. Geological survey of New Jersey: Geological Survey.

Gertler E. 1992. *Garden State canoeing: a paddler's guide to New Jersey.* Phoenix (AZ): Seneca Press.

Gillis CA, Bonnevie NL, Su SH, Ducey JG, Huntley SL, Wenning RJ. 1995. DDT, DDD, and DDE contamination of sediment in the Newark Bay Estuary, New Jersey. *Arch. Environ. Contam. Toxicol.* 28:85–92.

Goodman GT, Edwards RW, Lambert JM, editors. 1965. *Ecology and the industrial society. British Ecological Society Symposium Number Five.* Oxford [Eng.]: Blackwell Scientific Publications.

Griscom L. 1929. Changes in the status of certain birds in the New York City region. *Auk* 46:45–57.

Gunster DG, Bonnevie NL Gillis CA, Wenning RJ. 1993. Assessment of chemical loadings to Newark Bay, New Jersey from petroleum and hazardous chemical accidents occurring from 1986 to 1991. *Ecotoxicol. Environ. Safety* 25:202–213.

Havlick SW. 1974. *The urban organism.* New York: Macmillan Publishing Co., Inc.

Hawley A. 1971. *Urban society: an ecological approach.* New York: The Ronald Press Company.

Headlee TJ. 1935. *The New Jersey mosquito problem: a survey of past performance, present state, and future outlook.* New Brunswick (NJ): New Jersey Agricultural Experiment Station.

Headlee TJ. 1945. *The mosquitoes of New Jersey and their control.* New Brunswick (NJ): Rutgers University Press.

Headlee TJ, Carroll M. 1919. *The mosquito must go.* New Brunswick (NJ): New Jersey Agricultural Experiment Station.

Heusser CJ. 1963. Pollen diagrams from three former cedar bogs in the Hackensack tidal marsh, northeastern New Jersey. *Bulletin of the Torrey Botanical Club* 90(1):16–28.

Hine CG. 1909. *Woodside: the north end of Newark, NJ: its history, legends, and ghost stories gathered from the records and the older inhabitants now living.* Hine's Annual.

Holmes H. 1885. *A brief history of Belleville.*

Holmes H. 1890. *Reminiscences of 75 years of Belleville, Franklin and Newark.* Second edition.

Huntley SL, Bonnevie NL, Wenning RJ, Bedbury H. 1993. Distribution of polycyclic aromatic hydrocarbons (PAHs) in three northern New Jersey waterways. *Bull. Environ. Contam. Toxicol.* 51:865–872.

Huntley SL, Bonnevie NL, Wenning RJ. 1995. Polycyclic aromatic hydrocarbon and petroleum hydrocarbon contamination in sediment from the Newark Bay Estuary, New Jersey. *Arch. Environ. Contam. Toxicol.* 28:93–107.

Huntley SL, Iannuzzi TJ, Avantaggio JD, Carlson-Lynch H, Schmidt CW, Finley BL. 1997. Combined sewer overflows (CSOs) as sources of sediment contamination in the lower Passaic River, New Jersey. II. Polychlorinated dibenzo-*p*-dioxins, polychlorinated dibenzofurans, and polychlorinated biphenyls. *Chemosphere* 34(2):233–250.

Hurley A. 1992. Oil and water. *Seaport* 26:14–21.

HydroQual. 1995. *Assessment of pollutant loadings in New York-New Jersey Harbor.* Prepared for U.S. Environmental Protection Agency, 1991 Jan.

Iannuzzi TJ, Wenning RJ. 1995. Distribution and possible sources of total mercury in sediments from the Newark Bay Estuary, New Jersey. *Bull. Environ. Contam. Toxicol.* 55:901–908.

Iannuzzi TJ, Huntley SL, Bonnevie NL, Finley BL, Wenning RJ. 1995. Distribution of possible sources of polychlorinated biphenyls in dated sediments from the Newark Bay estuary, New Jersey. *Arch. Environ. Contam. Toxicol.* 28:108–117.

Iannuzzi TJ, Harrington NW, Shear NM, Curry CL, Carlson-Lynch H, Henning MH, Su SH, Rabbe DE. 1996. Distributions of key exposure factors controlling the uptake of xenobiotic chemicals in an estuarine food web. *Environ. Toxicol. Chem.* 15(11):1979–1992.

Iannuzzi TJ, Huntley SL, Schmidt CW, Finley BL, McNutt RP, Burton SJ. 1997. Combined sewer overflows (CSOs) as sources of sediment contamination in the lower Passaic River, New Jersey. 1. Priority pollutants and inorganic chemicals. *Chemosphere* 34(2):213–231

Ingersoll E. 1887. The oyster, scallop, clam, mussel, and abalone industries. In: Goode GB, editor. *The fisheries and fishery industries of the United States, Section V: history and methods of the fisheries.* Washington DC: Government Printing Office.

ISC [Interstate Sanitation Commission]. 1939. *Annual report of the Interstate Sanitation Commission for the year 1939.* New York, NY.

IntraSearch. 1999. Wetland historical study, Hackensack River, New Jersey. IntraSearch Inc., Denver, CO, January.

Jacobson D. 1957. Origins of the town of Newark. *NJ History* 75:158–169.

Jacobson D. 1958. The pollution problem of the Passaic River. *Proceedings of the New Jersey Historical Society* 76:186–198.

Jenkinson RC. 1912. Newark Meadow reclamation situation. *Unknown newspaper source.*

JCWS [Joint Commission on the Water Supply]. 1873. *Reports to the Joint Commission on the water supply of the cities of Newark and Jersey City* [selected pages from the Chemical and Sanitary Report by Professor H. Wurtz]. Newark.

Kalm P. 1770. *Travels in North America. Vol. II.* New York: Wilson-Erickson, Inc.

Keller AA, Hinga KR, Oviatt CA. 1991. *New York-New Jersey Harbor estuary program module 4: nutrients and organic enrichment. Final report.* Marine Ecosystems Research Laboratory, University of Rhode Island. June 21.

Kennish MJ. 1992. *Ecology of estuaries: Anthropogenic effects.* Boca Raton (FL): CRC Press.

Kieran J. 1959. *A natural history of New York city.* First ed. Boston: Houghton Mifflin Company.

Killam ET. 1983. *The short-term and long-term impacts of combined sewer outflow discharges on the water quality of the lower Passaic River. Combined Sewer Overflow Facility Plan. Phase I, Volume 2.* In association with Najarian & Associates, Middletown and Milburn, New Jersey. Prepared for Passaic Valley Sewerage Commissioners.

Kneib RT. 1993. Growth and mortality in successive cohorts of fish larvae within an estuarine nursery. *Mar. Ecol. Prog. Ser.* 94:115–127.

Kneib RT. 1997. The role of tidal marshes in the ecology of estuarine nekton. *Oceanography and Marine Biology: An Annual Review* 35:163–220.

Kopp RJ, Smith VK (editors). 1993. *Valuing natural assets. The economics of natural resource damage assessment.* Washington, DC: Resources for the Future.

Kozlovsky DG. 1974. *An ecological and evolutionary ethic.* Englewood Cliffs, NJ: Prentice-Hall, Inc.

Kraft HC. 1986. *The Lanape, archaeology, history, and ethnography.* Newark (NJ): New Jersey Historical Society.

Kraus ML, Smith DJ. 1988. Competition and succession in a perturbed urban estuary: the effects of hydrology, p. 325–327. In: *Proceedings of the National Wetlands Symposium: Mitigation of Impacts and Losses;* New Orleans, LA, 1986 Oct 8–10.

Krech S, III. 1999. *The ecological Indian: myth and history.* First ed. New York: W.W. Norton & Company.

Kummel HB. 1908. *Geological Survey of New Jersey. U.S. Coast and Geodetic Survey with HB Kummel, NJ State Geologist. Two maps that show the former locations of salt marshes, freshwater marshes and streams along Newark Bay, the Passaic River, the Kill Van Kull, and the Hackensack River.* Washington: U.S. Geological Survey.

Kurien J. 1998. Traditional ecological knowledge and ecosystem sustainability: new meaning to Asian coastal proverbs. *Ecological Applications* 8(1) Supplemental S2-S5.

Lawrence GN. 1867. Catalogue of birds observed on New York, Long Island, Staten Island and adjacent parts of New Jersey. *Annals of the Lyceum of Natural History of New York* 8:279–300.

Leary PJ. 1891. *Newark, N.J., illustrated.* First ed. Newark, NJ: Wm. A. Baker.

Leck CF. 1984. *The status and distribution of New Jersey's birds.* New Brunswick, NJ: Rutgers University Press.

Lee FB. 1902. *New Jersey as a colony and as a state; one of the original thirteen.* New York: The Publishing Society of New Jersey.

Lee KN. 1993. *Compass and gyroscope: integrating science and politics for the environment.* Washington, DC: Island Press.

Leeds AR. 1887. *Shall we continue to use the sewage polluted Passaic or shall we get pure water?* NJ: Jersey City Printing Company.

Leffingwell FD. 1865. Map of the townships of Bloomfield and Belleville.

Leighton MO. 1902. *Sewage pollution in the metropolitan area near New York City and its effect on inland water resources.* U.S. Geological Survey-Water Supply Paper No. 72.

Ludwig D. 1985. The final frontier. *Bull. Ecol. Soc. Am.* 66:332–333.

Ludwig D. 1989. Anthropic ecosystems. *Bull Ecol. Soc. Am.* 70:12–14.

Lunny RM. 1959. *Juet's journal: the voyage of the* Half Moon *from 4 April to 7 November 1609.* Newark (NJ): The New Jersey Historical Society.

MacFarquhar N. 1995. A battle on the waterfront: conflicting visions for the renewal of the Passaic River. *New York Times* 1995 July 11, Metro Section.

MacKenzie CL Jr. 1992. *The fisheries of Raritan Bay.* New Brunswick (NJ): Rutgers University Press.

Macnab JA. 1890. *Song of the Passaic.* New York: Walbridge and Co.

Map of Essex County, NJ. 1997. Hagstrom Map Company, Inc.

McCay BJ. 1998. *Oyster wars and the public trust: property, law, and ecology in New Jersey history.* Tucson (AZ): University of Arizona Press.

McCormick JM, Quinn PT. 1975. Life in Newark Bay. *Underwater Naturalist* 9(1):12–14.

McCormick JM, Hires RI, Luther GW, Cheng SL. 1983. Partial recovery of

Newark Bay, NJ, following pollution abatement. *Mar. Poll. Bull.* 14(5):188–197.

McFadden E. 1962. Boating revival recalls heyday on Passaic: River once was center of rowing sport and social activities. *Newark News* 1962 Aug 19.

McHugh JL, Wise WM, Young RR. 1990. *Historical trends in the abundance and distribution of living marine resources.* Cleaning Up Our Coastal Waters: an Unfinished Agenda, at Riverdale, NY.

McKeever CK. 1941. Distribution and habitat selection of some local birds. *Proceedings of the Linnaean Society of New York* 52–53:84–112.

McKeever CK. 1946. New York City seabird colonies. *Proceedings of the Linnaean Society of New York* (54–57):46–47.

Metro Newark. 1981. Crew on the Passaic, school's reviving an old "shell game." *Metro Newark*, The Magazine of Northern New Jersey 1981 June/July Vol. XXVI, No. 3.

Meyerson AL, Luther GW III, Krajewski J, Hires RI. 1981. Heavy metal distribution in Newark Bay sediments. *Mar. Poll. Bull.* 12(7):244–250.

Michelson G. 1932. River's rowing days live only in memory: Some veterans still swing oars now and then, but younger men show no eagerness to try skill on Passaic. *Sunday Call* 1932 Sep17.

Minello TJ, Zimmerman RJ. 1991. The role of estuarine habitats in regulating growth and survival of juvenile penaeid shrimp, p. 1–16. In: DeLoach P, Dougherty WJ, Davidson MA, editors. *Frontiers in shrimp research.* Amsterdam: Elsevier Science Publishers B.V.

Mish FC, editor. 1994. *Merriam Webster's collegiate dictionary. 10th ed.* Springfield (MA): Merriam-Webster, Incorporated.

Mitchell B. 1970. Passaic River included among 10 most polluted in nation. *Newark Sunday News* 1970 Mar 22.

Mitsch WJ, Gosselink JG. 1993. *Wetlands.* Second ed. New York: Van Nostrand Reinhold.

Moran MA, Limburg KE. 1986. Introduction, p. 1–5. In: Limburg KE, Moran MA, McDowell WH, editors. *The Hudson River ecosystem.* New York: Springer-Verlag.

Morris LA, Bush PB, Clark JS. 1992. Ecological impacts and risks associated with forest management. Chapter 10, p. 119–152. In: Cairns J Jr., Niederlehner BR, Orvos DR (editors). *Predicting ecosystem risk.* Volume XX of Advances in Modern Environmental Toxicology series. Princeton NJ: Princeton Scientific Publishing Co., Inc.

Myers N, Simon JL. 1994. *Scarcity or abundance? A debate on the environment.* New York: W.W. Norton & Company.

NOAA [National Oceanic and Atmospheric Administration]. 1978. *Contaminant inputs to the New York Bight.* Pp 222. National Oceanic and Atmospheric Administration. NOAA Technical Memo ERL MESA-6; 1976.

NOAA [National Oceanic and Atmospheric Administration]. 1981. *Water quality of the Hudson-Raritan Estuary.* National Oceanic and Atmosphere Administration. Boulder, CO. NOAA Grant No. NA80RAD00034.

NOAA [National Oceanic and Atmospheric Administration]. 1984. *A geochemical assessment of sedimentation and contaminant distributions in the Hudson-Raritan Estuary.* Rockville, MD: NOAA, National Ocean Service.

NOAA [National Oceanic and Atmospheric Administration]. 1996. *Natural resource restoration plan for oil and chemical resources in the New York/New Jersey Harbor Estuary [Draft].* New York: Prepared jointly by NOAA, NYSDEC, NJDEP, NY City Departments of Parks and Environmental Protection, and the USDOI.

Nereid Boat Club. 1999. Personal communication 1999 May 6. Coach of Nereid Boat Club and two rowers with Jason Kinnell and David Jefferson of Triangle Economic Research.

NJBFF [New Jersey Bureau of Freshwater Fisheries]. 1981. *Fish and wildlife resources and their supporting ecosystems: anadromous fish study of the Passaic River Basin, New Jersey.* Trenton: Prepared by the New Jersey Division of Fish, Game and Wildlife, Bureau of Freshwater Fisheries for the U.S. Fish and Wildlife Service.

NJDEP [New Jersey Department of Environmental Protection]. 1972–1980. *Lands now or formerly below mean high water: overlay preparation summary.* Trenton, (NJ): NJDEP, Tidelands Management Program.

NJDEP [New Jersey Department of Environmental Protection]. 1980. *A comprehensive monitoring and assessment program for selected heavy metals in New Jersey aquatic fauna.* NJDEP, New Jersey Marine Sciences Consortium, June 1980.

NJDEP [New Jersey Department of Environmental Protection]. 1982. Index.

Lands subject to investigation for areas now or formerly below mean high water. Prepared for the Tidelands Resource Council. Prepared by the State of New Jersey, Department of Environmental Protection, office of Environmental Analysis. April 1982.

NJDEP [New Jersey Department of Environmental Protection]. 1983. *PCBs in selected finfish caught within New Jersey waters 1981–1982 (with limited chlordane data)*. NJDEP, Office of Science and Research, July 1983.

NJDEP [New Jersey Department of Environmental Protection]. 1985a. *A study of toxic hazards to urban recreational fishermen and crabbers*. NJDEP, Office of Science and Research, September 1985.

NJDEP [New Jersey Department of Environmental Protection]. 1985b. *A study of dioxin in aquatic animals and sediments*. NJDEP, Office of Science and Research, October 1985.

NJDEP [New Jersey Department of Environmental Protection]. 1987. *Passaic River water quality management study*. Trenton, (NJ): NJDEP, Division of Water Resources, Bureau of Water Quality Standards and Analysis, April 1987.

NJDEP [New Jersey Department of Environmental Protection]. 1990. *Polychlorinated biphenyls (PCBs), chlordane, and DDTs in selected fish and shellfish from New Jersey waters, 1986–1987: results from New Jersey's toxics in biota monitoring program*. NJDEP, Office of Science and Research.

NJDEP [New Jersey Department of Environmental Protection]. 1993. *Polychlorinated biphenyls (PCBs), chlordane, and DDTs in selected fish and shellfish from New Jersey waters, 1988–1991: results from New Jersey's toxics in biota monitoring program*. NJDEP, Office of Science and Research, July 1993.

NJDEP [New Jersey Department of Environmental Protection]. 1999. Personal communication with David Jefferson, Triangle Economic Research, 1999 Feb 24. New Jersey Department of Environmental Protection, Division of Science and Research.

NJDEP [New Jersey Department of Environmental Protection], NJDHSS [New Jersey Department of Health & Senior Services]. 1997. *A guide to health advisories for eating fish and crabs caught in New Jersey waters: what you need to know about recreational fishing and crabbing*. NJDEP and NJDHSS.

NJMSC [New Jersey Marine Sciences Consortium]. 1987. *The Hudson-Raritan: State of the estuary, Summary. Vol. 1, Part 1*. Report by the Panel on Water

Quality of the Hudson-Raritan Estuary, New Jersey Marine Sciences Consortium.

New Jersey State Museum. 1903. *Annual report of the New Jersey State Museum, including a list of the birds of New Jersey, with a description of each, and illustrations, and the law protecting birds, etc.* Trenton: New Jersey State Museum.

New Jersey State Planning Board. 1937. *A map of fish and game resources of New Jersey showing wooded and marsh areas.* Trenton, NJ.

New Jersey State Planning Board. 1939. *Where shall we play?* A report on the outdoor recreational needs of New Jersey. Trenton, NJ.

NY/NJ HEP [New York/New Jersey Harbor Estuary Program]. 1996. *New York - New Jersey Harbor Estuary Program Final Comprehensive Conservation and Management Plan.*

Newark Athletic Club News. 1921. The putrid Passaic pellucid again. *Newark Athletic Club News* 1921 Feb.

Newark Daily Advertiser. 1866. The Passaic boat club. *Newark Daily Advertiser* 1866 May 24.

Newark Evening News. 1934. Photograph of Passaic fishing expedition, p22. *Newark Evening News* 1934 May 18.

Newark News. 1905. The Passaic River as it was of old: How the picturesque river appeared to the youth of forty-five years ago. *Newark News* 1905.

Newark News. 1915. Yacht club opens new sub-station. *Newark News* 1915 Sep 20.

Newark News. 1933a. Crowds of swimmers using Passaic River, p. 1, col. 7. *Newark News* 1933 May 26.

Newark News. 1933b. Equal rights, why can't boys swim in Passaic River? Fish do, p. 19, col. 3. *Newark News* 1933 June 14.

Newark News. 1936a. Heat tide brings changed living habits. *Newark News* 1936 July.

Newark News. 1936b. Nereid Oarsmen to compete in Passaic regatta Sunday, p. 25, col. 3. *Newark News* 1936 Sep 16.

Newark News. 1936c. Nudists in the Passaic. *Newark News* 1936 Sep 26.

Newark News. 1938. Boats in river tossed by storm. Newark News 1938 Sep 22; p 30 (col 8).

Newark News. 1940. Boatman lives out saga of 128 years on Passaic. *Newark News* 1940 Dec 4.

Newark News. 1946. Summer smiles on Passaic but North Arlington and Sewer Board can't because river remains unclean. *Newark News* 1946 Aug 5.

Newark News. 1948. Sewerage Commission to purify river. *Newark News* 1948 Nov 7.

Newark News. 1956. They hold fast to hope for a beautiful Passaic. *Newark News* 1956 Apr 22.

Noble RE. 1959. Four Wilson campaign speeches [selected pages]. *New Jersey History* 77(2):76–79.

Odum E. 1963. *Ecology.* New York: Holt, Rinehart and Winston, Inc.

Paling JE. 1971. Causes of mortality, p. 249–258. In: Ricker WE, editor. *Methods for assessment of fish production in fresh waters.* Oxford (Eng): Blackwell Scientific Publications.

Parsons KC. 1993. The Arthur Kill oil spills: biological effects to birds. In Burger J. editor. *The Arthur Kill. Anatomy of an oil spill.* New Brunswick: Rutgers University Press.

Passaic River Coalition. 1983. PRRP tours lower Passaic. *Goals and Strategies Newsletter* Summer 1983.

Passaic River Coalition. 1984. Debris to go!!! *Goals and Strategies Newsletter* Summer 1984.

Passaic River Coalition. 1987. Passaic River restoration project master plan. *Garfield Harrison Revisions* 1987.

Passaic Valley Sewerage Commission. 1897. *Report of the Passaic Valley Sewerage Commission upon the general system of sewage disposal for the valley of the Passaic River, and the prevention of the pollution thereof.* Newark: John E. Rowe & Son Printers; 1897 Feb.

Peet J, Johnson T. 1996. The forgotten river. *Star-Ledger* 1996 Aug 18–20 Three Part Series.

Percival RV, Miller AS, Schroeder CH, Leape JP. 1992. *Environmental regulation: law, science and policy.* Boston: Little, Brown and Company.

Pflug KK. 1996. The hidden dangers in urban fish. *New Jersey Outdoors* 1996 Fall:54–57.

Pianka ER. 1974. *Evolutionary ecology.* 1st Edition. New York: Harper and Row, Publishers.

Pierce B, Patterson C, Gerdes FH. 1874. *U.S. coast survey of the Hackensack and Passaic Rivers and vicinity, 1871 and 1874.*

Pierson DL. 1917. *Narratives of Newark (in New Jersey)*. Newark (NJ): Pierson Publishing Co.

Platt RH, Rowntree RA, Muick PC. 1994. *The ecological city: preserving and restoring urban biodiversity*. Amherst: Univ. of Massachusetts Press.

Pomeroy LR, Wiegart RG (editors). 1981. *The ecology of a salt marsh*. New York: Springer-Verlag, Inc.

Ponting C. 1991. *A green history of the world: the environment and the collapse of great civilizations*. New York: Penguin.

Prial FJ. 1961. Woodside had rustic charm. *Newark Sunday News* 1961 June 3.

Princeton University Students. 1971. *Water pollution in the Passaic River basin, New Jersey: analysis of problems and recommendations for possible solutions*. Prepared by students in the student-initiated seminar: Technology and Society: Problems in the Human Environment. Princeton University School of Engineering and Applied Science, Department of Civil and Geological Engineering. January.

Pyne SJ. 1997a. *Fire in America: a cultural history of wildland and rural fire*. Seattle: University of Washington Press.

Pyne SJ. 1997b. *Vestal fire: an environmental history, told through fire, of Europe and Europe's encounter with the world*. Seattle: University of Washington Press.

Pyne SJ. 1997c. *World fire: the culture of fire on earth*. Seattle: University of Washington Press.

Pyne SJ. 1998. *Burning bush: a fire history of Australia*. Seattle: University of Washington Press.

Quinn JR. 1997. *Fields of sun and grass: an artist's journal of the New Jersey meadowlands*. New Brunswick (NJ): Rutgers University Press.

Quinn JR. 1998. The fishes swim through it—once again. In: *Fishes of the Hackensace River Estuary*, July 1998.

Rankin ES. 1918. *Historical map of Newark, New Jersey 1666–1916*. Compiled for the 250th Anniversary Celebration by ES Rankin. Revised, corrected and published for the Board of Education for use in the Public Schools.

Rankin ES. 1927. *Indian trails and city streets*. Montclair (NJ): The Globe Press.

Rankin E. 1930. *The Running Brooks and other sketches of early Newark*. Somerville (NJ): Unionist-Gazette.

Rapp. 1998. Personal communication 1998 July 13. Proprietor of Rapp's Boatyard with Rick Dunford and Jason Kinnell of Triangle Economic Research.

Redman CL. 1999. *Human impact on ancient environments*. Tucson: The University of Arizona Press.

Rod SR, Ayres RU, et al. 1989. *Final report to the Hudson River Foundation: reconstruction of historical loadings of heavy metals and chlorinated hydrocarbon pesticides in the Hudson-Raritan Basin, 1880–1980*. Pittsburgh [PA], Carnegie Mellon University, Department of Engineering and Public Policy.

Rogers GF, Rowntree RA. 1988. Intensive surveys of structure and change in urban natural areas. *Landscape & Urban Planning* 15:59–78.

Rozas LP, Odum WE. 1987. Use of tidal freshwater marshes by fishes and macrofaunal crustaceans along a marsh stream-order gradient. *Estuaries* 10(1):36–43.

Russell EWB. 1980. Vegetational change in northern New Jersey from precolonization to the present: a palynological interpretation. *Bulletin of the Torrey Botanical Club* 107(3):432–446.

Santoro ED, Funicelli NA, Koepp SJ. 1980. Fishes of Newark Bay, NJ. *Underwater Naturalist* 12(2):22.

Scarlett and Scarlett. 1889. *Atlas of the City of Newark, New Jersey*. Newark.

Shaw W. 1884. *History of Essex and Hudson Counties, New Jersey*. Philadelphia: Everts & Peck.

Shear NM, Schmidt CW, Huntley SL, Crawford DW, Finley BL. 1996. Evaluation of the factors relating combined sewer overflows with sediment contamination of the lower Passaic River. *Marine Poll. Bull.* 32(3):288–304.

Shenker JM, Dean JM. 1979. The utilization of an intertidal salt marsh creek by larval and juvenile fishes: abundance, diversity and temporal variation. *Estuaries* 2(3):154–163.

Shriner CA. 1896. *The birds of New Jersey*. State of New Jersey Fish and Game Commission.

Siebenheller N. 1981. *Breeding birds of Staten Island, 1881-1981 (Including Shooter's Island, Prall's Island, Hoffman and Swinburne Islands)*. Staten Island: Staten Island Institute of Arts and Sciences.

Siebenheller W, Siebenheller N. 1983. Recent additions to "Breeding Birds of Staten Island 1881–1981." *Proceedings of the Staten Island Institute of Arts and Sciences* 32(1):1–3.

Literature Cited

Sigler WF, Sigler JW. 1990. *Recreational fisheries: management, theory, and application.* Reno: University of Nevada Press.

Sipple WS. 1972. The past and present flora and vegetation of the Hackensack Meadows. *Bartonia* (Journal of the Philadelphia Botanical Club) 41:4–56.

Smith S. 1887. Catalogue of the mollusca of Staten Island. *Proceedings of the Natural Science Association of Staten Island 2.*

Smith A. 1937. *The wealth of nations.* New York: Modern Library.

Sparks RE. 1992. Risks of altering the hydrologic regime of large rivers. Chapter 9, p. 119–152. In: Cairns J Jr., Niederlehner BR, Orvos DR (editors). *Predicting ecosystem risk.* Volume XX of Advances in Modern Environmental Toxicology series. Princeton NJ: Princeton Scientific Publishing Co., Inc.

Squires DF. 1981. *The bight of the big apple.* The New York Sea Grant Institute of the State University of New York and Cornell University.

Squires DF. 1992. Quantifying anthropogenic shoreline modification of the Hudson River and Estuary from European contact to modern time. *Coastal Management* 20:343–354.

Squires DF, Barclay JS. 1990. *Nearshore wildlife habitats and populations in the New York/New Jersey Harbor Estuary.* The University of Connecticut: Storrs, Marine Sciences Institute and Department of Natural Resources Management and Engineering.

Star-Ledger. 1929. Newark of other days—Passaic boat club. *Star-Ledger* 1929 Mar 30.

Star-Ledger. 1939. River patrol cops to stop swimming in Passaic. *Star-Ledger* 1939 July 23.

Star-Ledger. 1946. Water pollution: agencies gain in fight to purify NJ area. *Star-Ledger* 1946 July 20.

Stearns F, Montag T, editors. 1974. *The urban ecosystem: a holistic perspective.* Stroudsburg [PA]: Dowden, Hutchison & Ross, Inc.

Steimle FW, Caracciolo-Ward J. 1989. A reassessment of the status of benthic macrofauna of the Raritan Estuary. *Estuaries* 12(3):145–156.

Stickle WB, Kapper MA, et al. 1989. Metabolic adaptations of several species of crustaceans and mollusks to hypoxia: tolerances and microcalometric studies. *Biol. Bull.* 177:303–312.

Stone WJ. 1839. *Survey—Newark Bay*. Washington DC: Secretary of the Treasury.

Strims J. 1795. Map of Belleville [Sketch shows Green Island, Passaic River and First River/Mill Brook].

Sullivan R. 1998. *The Meadowlands: wilderness adventures at the edge of a city*. New York: Scribner.

Suszkowski DJ. 1978. *Sedimentology of Newark Bay, New Jersey: an urban estuarine bay*. Marine Studies, University of Delaware, pp 222.

Talbot CW, Able KW, Shisler JK. 1986. Fish species composition in New Jersey salt marshes: Effects of marsh alterations for mosquito control. *Trans. Am. Fish. Soc.* 115:269–278.

Teal J, Teal M. 1969. *Life and death of the salt marsh*. New York: Ballantine Books.

The Board of Education for the Study of Newark in the Schools of Newark, NJ. 1914. *The True Story of the Passaic River*. Leaflet No. 30.

The Record. 1987. Resurrecting the Passaic River. *The Record* 1987 June 29.

The Sunday Call. 1902. How would you enjoy being a figurehead on the polluted Passaic? *The Sunday Call* 1902 Jan 5.

The Sunday Call. 1936. Boy diving into the Passaic River. *The Sunday Call* 1936 July 12.

Torrey J. 1819. *Catalogue of plants, growing spontaneously within thirty miles of the City of New York*. Commissioned by the Lyceum of Natural History of New York. Albany (NJ): Websters and Skinners.

Urner CA. 1921. Short-eared owl nesting at Elizabeth, NJ. *Auk* 38:602–603.

Urner CA. 1923. Notes on the short-eared owl. *Auk* 40:30–36.

Urner CA. 1925. Notes on two ground-nesting birds of prey. *Auk* 42:31–41.

Urner CA. 1935. Relation of mosquito control in New Jersey marshes to bird life of the salt marshes. *Proceedings of the Twenty-Second Annual Meeting of the New Jersey Mosquito Extermination Association*; Atlantic City, NJ.

Urquhart FJ. 1913. *A history of the City of Newark, New Jersey, embracing practically two and a half centuries 1666–1913. Volume I*. The Lewis Historical Publishing Co.

USACE [U.S. Army Corps of Engineers]. 1880. *Annual report of the Chief of Engineers, U.S. Army, Appendix E, improvement of rivers in northern New Jersey*. Washington, DC.

USACE [U.S. Army Corps of Engineers]. 1884. *Annual report of the Chief of Engineers, U.S. Army, Appendix G8, improvement of the Passaic River above Newark, New Jersey*. Washington DC.

USACE [U.S. Army Corps of Engineers]. 1900. *Annual Reports of the War Department. Report of the Chief of Engineers. Part 2, Appendix H.* Washington, DC.

USACE [U.S. Army Corps of Engineers]. 1907. *Newark Bay, and Hackensack and Passaic Rivers, NJ.* Letter from the Secretary of War, 59th Congress, 2d Session, Washington, DC. House of Representatives Document No. 441, 1907 Jan 8.

USACE [U.S. Army Corps of Engineers]. 1912. *Newark Bay, and Hackensack and Passaic Rivers, NJ.* Letter from the Secretary of War, 62d Congress, 2d Session, Washington, DC. House of Representatives Document No. 707, 1912 Apr 18.

USACE [U.S. Army Corps of Engineers]. 1913. *Improvement of rivers and harbors in the northeastern New Jersey. Annual Report of the Chief of Engineers. Part 2, Appendix G.* Washington, DC.

USACE [U.S. Army Corps of Engineers]. 1914. *Improvement of rivers and harbors in the northeastern New Jersey. Annual Report of the Chief of Engineers. Part 2, Appendix G.* Washington, DC.

USACE [U.S. Army Corps of Engineers]. 1915. *Improvement of rivers and harbors in the third New York, NY, district. Annual Report of the Chief of Engineers. Part 2, Appendix G.* Washington, DC.

USACE [U.S. Army Corps of Engineers]. 1916. *Improvement of rivers and harbors in the third New York, NY district. Annual Report of the Chief of Engineers. Part 2, Appendix G.* Washington, DC.

USACE [U.S. Army Corps of Engineers]. 1917. *Improvement of rivers and harbors in the third New York, NY district. Annual Report of the Chief of Engineers. Part 2, Appendix G.* Washington, DC.

USACE [U.S. Army Corps of Engineers]. 1922. *Newark Bay, and Hackensack and Passaic Rivers, NJ.* Letter from the Secretary of War, 67th Congress, 2d Session, Washington, DC. House of Representatives Document No. 206, 1922 Mar 9.

USACE [U.S. Army Corps of Engineers]. 1953. *Waterborne commerce of the*

189

United States, NY District. Obtained from U.S. Army Corps Chief of Engineers Library, Washington DC.

USACE [U.S. Army Corps of Engineers]. 1966. *Newark Bay, and Hackensack and Passaic Rivers, NJ.* Letter from the Secretary of War, 89th Congress, 2d Session, Washington, DC. House of Representatives Document No. 494, 1966 Sep 12.

USACE [U.S. Army Corps of Engineers]. 1980. *Waterborne commerce of the United States, NY District.* Obtained from U.S. Army Corps Chief of Engineers Library, Washington DC.

USACE [U.S. Army Corps of Engineers]. 1987. *Passaic River Basin, New Jersey and New York. Phase I - general design memorandum. Flood protection feasibility main stem Passaic River. Main Report Appendix B - natural resources.* New York: U.S. Army Corps of Engineers.

USACE [U.S. Army Corps of Engineers]. 1997. *Waterborne commerce of the United States, waterways and harbors Atlantic coast.* Obtained from http://www.wrsc.usace.army.mil/ ndc/wcusatl.pdf.

U.S. Coast Guard Bridge Administration. 1984. *Bridges over navigable waters of the United States, Atlantic Coast.* Received from Yee J, U.S. Coast Guard Bridge Administration; 1984 May; P16590.1.

U.S. Coast Guard Bridge Administration. 1997. 33 CFR ß117.739 Passaic River, Ch. 1, 1997 July 1).

U.S. Department of Commerce. 1990. *Passaic and Hackensack Rivers Map.* U. S. Department of Commerce, National Oceanic and Atmospheric Administration, National Ocean Service, 21st ed. (13 October 1990), 12337.

USEPA [U.S. Environmental Protection Agency]. 1994. *Revised community relations plan, Passaic River study area Diamond Alkali Superfund site, Essex and Hudson Counties, NJ.* USEPA, 1994 May.

USEPA [U.S. Environmental Protection Agency]. 1999. *National priority site fact sheet.* Available from: http://www.epa.gov/region02/Superfund/site_sum/ 0200613c.htm.

USEPA [U.S. Environmental Protection Agency], USACE [U.S. Army Corps of Engineers]. 1995. *Draft environmental impact statement on the Special Area Management Plan for the Hackensack Meadowlands District, NJ.* Prepared by the U.S. Environmental Protection Agency and the U.S. Army Corps of Engineers in cooperation with the National Atmospheric and Oceanic Administration, the New Jersey Department of Environmental Protection, and the Hackensack Meadowlands Development Commission.

Van Cleef JT, Betts, JB. 1887. *Map of the rail roads of New Jersey.*

Van Deventer F. 1964. *Cruising New Jersey tidewater: a boating and touring guide.* New Brunswick (NJ): Rutgers University Press.

Van Duyne & Sherman. 1868. Fire insurance map of Newark, New Jersey. Newark.

Van Winkle EH. 1847. *Topographical map of Newark, New Jersey.* Publisher unknown.

Vermeule CC. 1896. *Drainage of the Hackensack and Newark tide-marshes. Annual Report State Geologist, New Jersey Geological Survey 1863–1915.* Trenton: MacCrellish & Quigley.

Vernburg FJ. 1993. Salt-marsh processes: a review. *Environ. Toxicol. Chem.* 12: 2167–2195.

Wacker PO, Clemens PGE. 1995. *Land use in early New Jersey: a historical geography.* Newark (NJ): New Jersey Historical Society.

Waldman J. 1999. *Heartbeats in the muck: the history, sea life, and environment of New York Harbor.* First ed. New York: The Lyons Press.

Walker WJ, McNutt RP, Maslanka CK. 1999. The potential contribution of urban runoff to surface sediments of the Passaic River: sources and chemical characteristics. *Chemosphere* 38(2):363–377.

Walz T. 1993. River revival: 20-year cleanup plan paying off. *Sunday Record* 1993 February 14, A33.

Weisberg SB, Lotrich VA. 1982. The importance of an infrequently flooded intertidal marsh surface as an energy source for the mummichog *Fundulus heteroclitus*: an experimental approach. *Mar. Biol.* 66:307–310.

Wenning RJ, Harris MA, Finley B, Paustenbach DJ, Bedbury H. 1993a. Application of pattern recognition techniques to evaluate polychlorinated dibenzo-*p*-dioxin and dibenzofuran distributions in surficial sediments from the lower Passaic River and Newark Bay. *Ecotoxicol. Environ. Safety* 25:103–125.

Wenning R, Paustenbach D, Johnson G, Ehrlich R, Harris M, Bradbury H. 1993b. Chemometric analysis of potential sources of polychlorinated dibenzo-*p*-dioxins and dibenzofurans in surfical sediments from Newark Bay, New Jersey. *Chemosphere* 27(1–3):55–64.

Wenning RJ, Paustenbach, DJ, Harris MA, Bedbury H. 1993c. Principal components analysis of potential sources of polychlorinated dibenzo-*p*-dioxin and dibenzofuran residues in surficial sediments from Newark Bay, New Jersey. *Arch. Environ. Contam. Toxicol.* 24:271–289.

Wenning RJ, NL Bonnevie, SL Huntley. 1994. Accumulation of metals, polychlorinated biphenyls, and polycyclic aromatic hydrocarbons in sediments from the lower Passaic River, New Jersey. *Arch. Environ. Contam. Toxicol.* 27: 64–81.

White I. 1953. Jans club oarsmen wore odd duds. *Newark News* 1953 Mar 29.

Wildes HE. 1943. Twin rivers: the Raritan and the Passaic. New York: Farrar & Rinehart, Inc.

Williams WC. 1938. *Life along the Passaic River.* Norfolk (CT): New Directions.

Wright K. 1988. *The Hackensack Meadowlands: prehistory and history.* Prepared for the Hackensack Meadowlands Development Commission. Lyndhurst.

INDEX

Index